everything

you ever needed to know about

training

I would like to dedicate this fourth edition to the person who constantly inspires me, who is my source of energy and imagination and is my best friend.
Kaye Thorne

To my mother who ensured that I understood the value of learning and to my wife Sally who has provided the inspiration and time to allow me to complete this book.
David Mackey

everything

you ever needed to know about

training

4th edition

A one-stop shop for everyone interested in training, learning and development

kaye thorne   david mackey

KOGAN
PAGE

London and Philadelphia

Publisher's note

Every possible effort has been made to ensure that the information contained in this book is accurate at the time of going to press, and the publishers and authors cannot accept responsibility for any errors or omissions, however caused. No responsibility for loss or damage occasioned to any person acting, or refraining from action, as a result of the material in this publication can be accepted by the editor, the publisher or either of the authors.

First published in Great Britain and the United States in 2007 by Kogan Page Limited

120 Pentonville Road
London N1 9JN
United Kingdom
www.kogan-page.co.uk

525 South 4th Street, #241
Philadelphia PA 19147
USA

© Kaye Thorne and David Mackey, 2007

The right of Kaye Thorne and David Mackey to be identified as the authors of this work has been asserted by them in accordance with the Copyright, Designs and Patents Act 1988.

ISBN-10   0 7494 5008 8
ISBN-13   978 0 7494 5008 3

British Library Cataloguing-in-Publication Data

A CIP record for this book is available from the British Library.

Library of Congress Cataloging-in-Publication Data

Thorne, Kaye.
  Everything you ever needed to know about training / Kaye Thorne and David Mackey. -- 4th ed.
    p. cm.
  Includes index.
  ISBN-13: 978-0-7494-5008-3
  ISBN-10: 0-7494-5008-8
  1. Employees--Training of. 2. Organizational learning. I. Mackey, David. II. Title.
  HF5549.5.T7T4625 2007
  658.3'124--dc22
                              2007011091

Typeset by Jean Cussons Typesetting, Diss, Norfolk
Printed and bound in India by Replika Press Pvt Ltd

Contents

Acknowledgements

In a lifetime of learning we have met many people who have contributed to our own learning. Particular influences are David A Kolb, Tony Buzan, Daniel Goleman and John Seymour, and the other authors mentioned in our bibliography.

Specifically in the development of this fourth edition we should like to thank the following:

- Mark Woodhouse for his wisdom and for all the creative and imaginative opportunities to develop Learning and Development and Training Excellence on a global basis.

- Chris Dunn, TDA Transitions Ltd, for sharing his vision, imagination and entrepreneurship in the development of a leading example of an innovative training business.

- Andy Pellant of Emergent Edge for his inspiration, personal support and creative challenges in the development of personalized learning.

- Ann Elliot, Alison Widdowson and the whole HR team at the Portman Building Society for their imaginative projects, creative HR strategies and their ongoing support and friendship.

- We also acknowledge the work of those who created the models and concepts that underpin many T&D activities, eg SMART. David A Kolb for the inspiration behind *How People Learn* and for permission to reproduce his Experiential Learning Model. Tony Buzan for his innovative Mind Map Method®. Peter Honey and Alan Mumford for the Learning Styles questionnaire.

- Roger Greenwood, Esprit, Richard Graham, Huthwaite, and Dermot Bradley – three inspirational leaders in UK sales training.
- Paul Ewins and Phil Dennis, HSBC Bank plc; Chris George of Styles & George; Trevor Tribe and Philip Mason of MacIntyre Hudson for financial support and advice.
- All the staff at the CIPD and IOD Libraries for their very professional and responsive help in compiling the bibliography and the international training contacts.
- Suzi Yousif and Brian Hayer for their helpful subject expert advice for Chapter 8.

All authors need support and we owe a particular debt of gratitude to the following for their encouragement and interest.

Kelvin Harris, Matt, Lesley and Luke Thorne, and Louise, Mark, Charlotte and Annabelle Sinclair for their love, inspiration and generosity of spirit.

Vivien Dunn, Barbara Bonner, Carolin Garside and the whole TDA team of staff and associates, for their professionalism, dedication and support. Bob North and a fine team of trainers, supporting staff and associates at Thales Training and Consultancy. Brenda Myrans and the team at Learning & Development, LogicaCMG. The following good friends and colleagues for their ongoing support and inspiration: Alex Machray, Keith Bastin, Kevin McGrath, Alan Stanhope, John Kenney, Paul Allen, Cheri Lofland, Doug and Lisa Twining, Alan Smith, Sheena Matthews, Ian Banyard, Llorett Kemplen, Sid and Elizabeth Cole, Bernice Legg, Ian and Rosemary Anderson, Rob and Sue Ford, Bill Eldridge, Keith Harriss, Ian McKenzie, Al Dunn, Siân Livsey, Margaret Burnside, Mike Brewer and John Kilvington. The Kilby family and staff at the Garrack Hotel, St Ives, Cornwall, for providing an inspirational environment in which to write.

Charlotte Atyeo, Viki Williams and Heather Langridge, our editors, and all those who have worked on previous editions, for their refreshing approach to publishing and for providing superb technical support and advice.

But above all, the very special clients and individual learners who ultimately have been our inspiration, and without whom this book would never have been written, our particular thanks to you.

Preface to the fourth edition

Welcome to the fourth edition of *Everything You Ever Needed to Know About Training*. It's 10 years since the first edition was published, and much has changed in the world of training since then. Here are some of the changes:

- Training departments in many large organizations have greatly reduced.

- In many organizations training, learning and development have become part of larger Human Resources departments.

- Some organizations have developed their own in-company academies/universities.

- Increased legislation has meant that many professionals within HR are spending greater amounts of time on protecting the business rather than developing people.

- Outsourcing has increased with different parts of HR and training being handled by outside contractors.

- The roles within HR have become more diverse with descriptors such as business partner, eHR manager, HR adviser, HR shared services manager, learning and development manager, career development manager, reward manager and change manager, which is a long way from the traditional roles of training and personnel.

- New terms have developed: emotional intelligence, employer branding, employee engagement, business partnering, talent management, diversity, e-learning, blended learning, thought leadership and knowledge management, which didn't exist 10 years ago, or if they did exist were not well-known.

Through the different editions we have tried to include developments as they have occurred, but at this time of the 10th anniversary of the publication it is interesting to reflect on how training has developed during that time.

We are also aware that this book has been translated into different languages, and is available globally. We also know that the facilities that are available to learning professionals vary enormously, from the most sophisticated state-of-the-art learning studios to a storeroom, or small office above the shop for some small businesses. Whatever the environment, or the availability of equipment, the focus should be about creating a learning experience that meets the needs of the learner and is delivered with passion and enthusiasm.

Training equipment is also evolving, and we have tried to incorporate the latest terminology, although we also recognize that some people are still using OHPs and projectors while others are using PDAs and podcasts, but it seems that flipcharts will run forever!

In terms of the learning agenda the list below represents some of the key areas that our colleagues have highlighted:

- 'Becoming an employer of choice and employee engagement.'
- 'The "war for talent", how to recruit, retain and succession plan.'
- 'Leading and managing change is a core capability for most organizations – the challenge is how to build and embed in the organization, and how important it is to have a consistent change methodology and underpinning tools.'
- 'Leadership models based on releasing potential and coaching.'
- 'Performance measures – where do organizations need/want to be world-class/best in class? What are the implications for capabilities required and the organization model to deliver?'
- 'How to really step up to being a true business partner. How to organize the delivery, and how to measure their "value add" to the business.'
- 'Increasing focus on cost – also means organizations are having to think about different ways of delivering learning.'
- 'The use of technology varies from organization to organization, particularly the "blended learning" debate, which has been problematical in terms of implementation for many organizations.'

- 'Outsourcing bubbles along for the more fundamental stuff.'
- 'Executive development still seems to be hanging on in there from a strategic perspective and linking this with corporate strategy and competency frameworks.'

We have incorporated this feedback into our revisions, particularly in certain key areas. 'E-learning' has evolved to become 'blended learning' and, to reflect this, we have updated the new chapter introduced in the second edition, 'Getting the best from E-learning', to include blended learning.

There has also been a continuation of the trend that we highlighted in the second edition: the reduction of traditional, menu-driven training courses, which have been replaced by a variety of learning solutions.

The role of the trainer has continued to evolve to include internal consultant, learning adviser, facilitator of learning, e-learning designer and workplace coach. Coaching in fact has grown considerably in significance, and to reflect this we have included a new section in 'The Trainer As...' chapter, specifically focusing on personal coaching. The scope, complexity and challenge of the trainer role are ever growing. Line managers have been encouraged to be more proactive in the training and development of their teams and, with many new aspects to training and learning, there are more opportunities for trainers to work in partnership with line managers.

Importantly one of the key development areas for trainers and development specialists is the ability to cope with ambiguity and to be able to respond rapidly to the needs of their customers. As one of the responses in our research above indicated, there is a very real need for internal training functions and any professionals engaged in working with an organization to be able to identify exactly what value they are adding and what their contribution as business partner is.

What is training?

You can run a very interesting half-hour session with a group by asking them to define training. Some of their responses may be as follows:

- 'It happens off-job.'
- 'It happens on-job.'
- 'It is showing someone how to do something.'
- 'It gives a set of objectives that the learner has to achieve.'

Training is often seen as something that is work-related – on-job training, off-job training, or employment training schemes. In many cases it is perceived as being a formal process, ie with a trainer in a training room, often supported by materials such as a delegate guide. The underpinning principles of how people learn, learning styles, listening, questioning and giving feedback apply to training as well as teaching, lecturing, coaching and assessing. There is normally an expectation that the training will have an aim and objectives, structured contents and evaluation.

Within this process there is an enormous range of variations in delivery depending on the style and approach of the trainer and the context of the training. At one end of the spectrum there are highly facilitative trainers who use very few formal inputs, relying on their experience to generate ideas within the group – they are very much output-driven. At the other end are the more traditional skills trainers, those who may be more comfortable in a 'tell' environment; their natural style is to input information. Both could be described as trainers delivering training, but the learning experience of the delegates will be very different in each case. Both approaches have advantages and disadvantages.

Facilitative trainers naturally work well with groups. Through their own personal creativity and energy they facilitate and encourage individuals and groups to excel. The more traditional trainers may find this approach difficult to emulate. They have to learn new behaviours, their style may be more directive or they are used to adopting an 'expert' role.

In training today there should be a combination of active participation and information giving. Delegates like to feel that the trainer has 'given' them something. It might be a model, a process or information. They don't want to feel that all the trainer has done is tell them what they already know. That gives substance to the old saying about consultants borrowing your watch to tell you the time and then charging you for the privilege.

Training itself is changing. Many traditional centres of skills training have disappeared and been replaced by distance learning resource centres, line manager coaching and special motivational training events off-site. With the development of blended learning, some training has been completely removed from a classroom environment and made available online. In some financial institutions and call centre environments training is very much linked to legislation, where consistency of delivery is essential. Today's organizations regard attendance at any training event as a serious investment that must provide value for money and relate to the objectives of the business. The term 'training' has evolved into 'learning and development'.

How to use this book

This book is about a journey, and the stages are clearly signposted so that you will reach your destination quickly. You may have travelled on some parts of the route before, and we anticipate you will wish only to look at the headings or checklists to ensure you are familiar with the content.

We hope you will find in the text everything you need to help you create exciting and interesting journeys for the learners with whom you work. The focus is on self-discovery and helping others enjoy the same delight and curiosity on their own development journey.

A book of this nature should provide connections to the larger world of learning. We hope that the information provided will help you find other more detailed books on specific topics highlighted in our text.

We have used 'he' and 'she' variously throughout to avoid gender bias.

The book gives key points and triggers that enable the beginner, as well as the more experienced trainer, to assimilate the concepts quickly and to develop individual pathways to learning. You can start reading at the beginning, the middle or the end.

It was very difficult to stop working on this book. Just when it seemed finished, another thought would occur to us or we would hear of some new development. That is how lifetime learning is: just when you think you know everything about a subject, somebody discovers something new. Learning is never static; it is constantly changing and adding new dimensions to your understanding of yourself or others. In this the fourth edition we have undertaken a broader review and included two new chapters, one on developing people and organizations and another on developing talent and employee engagement. We have also included other additions to reflect the changing world of training and development.

As with the earlier editions, this book is designed to highlight the key stages of identifying, designing and delivering learning and development that is dynamic, positive and challenging. Above all it is about recognizing that the quest for learning should never stand still – it is about sustaining curiosity and always seeking better ways of helping others to learn. In supporting that, it is about learning to encourage learners to have a thirst for knowledge, striving to be inspiring and inno-vative, and wanting to lead in the field of training and development.

We wish you every success in your continuing journey to inspiration.

You can contact us at kaye@theinspirationnetwork.co.uk and david@ ccfocus.co.uk. We look forward to hearing from you!

Developing People and Organizations

Before looking in detail at the role of a trainer, or learning and development professional, it is important to position training, learning and development in the context of an organization.

Increasingly individuals are thinking far more seriously about aligning their values to an organization's values, and so at recruitment they will look at what an organization can offer them as well as what they can offer an organization. The messages given through recruitment advertising and the recruitment process often have lasting effects on how an individual might view a company.

Becoming an employer of choice

Employer branding

One of the ways that organizations can align individual and organizational values is by becoming an employer of choice and a way of doing this is focusing on developing their employer brand. At its simplest form, employer branding is about ensuring that your people brand matches your marketing promises. In terms of brand management an aspirational goal for an organization should be that the marketing messages are reflected by the actions of all of the people at all levels of the business at all times in order to deliver the brand promise. To achieve that, however, you have to consider all aspects of your business to ensure consistency in your messages, behaviour and values.

Employee loyalty, commitment and performance = customer loyalty, advocacy and satisfaction = business growth, profitability and market share = stakeholder, competitor respect, employer of choice.

'Branding' as a generic term is often assumed to belong to the marketing function. Organizations, however, are realizing that directly or indirectly, people not products deliver most brand promises. In the broader context of employer branding it means the way organizations position themselves externally as well as internally. This will have particular relevance in the way organizations promote themselves in the recruitment marketplace, and in the way that they deal with customers. The people offer must match the marketing offer.

What is increasingly being recognized is that having strong consumer brands is not enough; organizations need to adopt an integrated approach encompassing:

- people;
- products/services;
- processes/systems;
- premises/environment.

As well as people and products, the underpinning infrastructure is important. When organizations re-engineer, or when new IT systems are being implemented, little time is allowed to prepare for the impact this can have on their people. Different departments simply do not communicate, or fail to realize the implication of their actions, and unfortunately HR are often the last people to be involved. Equally organizations may invest in the development of their customer-facing employees, but often do not apply the same principles to supporting the internal customer.

One way that HR/OD/L&D/Training departments can support organizations in becoming an employer of choice is to take a holistic view of development within an organization. We talk in Chapter 2 about being a business partner. A true business partner will have the ability to take an overview of the organization.

The development framework below highlights the key areas to cover; hopefully different parts of the framework will already be in place within your organization.

HR/OD/L&D/Training development framework

Our vision/mission/purpose

Where we want to be

This must be a real statement or statements that people can easily remember and identify with, not just words on a wall. It should be very clearly articulated, a test of its validity being that when asked, each and every employee clearly understands what the business is trying to achieve. Strongly identifying with the sentiment is more important that accuracy in the actual words. 'When people truly share a vision they are connected, bound together by a common aspiration' (Senge, 1990, *The Fifth Discipline*).

Our values

What we stand for/our integrity

Like vision, mission or purpose, an organization's values should run deep. The aim should be to encourage everyone to demonstrate the values through their behaviours; this particularly applies at senior level, when more junior employees are looking for role models.

In the current marketplace with increasing competition for talented employees, potential candidates are also trying to identify where the values of the organization are aligned with their own. Daniel Goleman, in his book *The New Leaders*, goes further when describing how to motivate employees, saying that:

> Getting people to really embrace change requires attunement, alignment with the kind of resonance that moves people emotionally as well as intellectually. Strategies couched as they often are in the dry language of corporate goals speak mainly to the rational brain, in the neocortex. Strategic visions and the plans that follow from them are typically linear and limited, bypassing the elements of heart and passion, essential for building commitment.

Behaviours, competencies, standards

What we demonstrate daily

This is a key area where cross-functional collaboration is essential. All too often the creation of the 'corporate way' is kept separate from the day-to-day measurement of individual performance. Employees need very clear guidance on the corporate expectations, eg this is the way we do things, the way our performance is measured; it applies to everyone and ensures consistency.

It has to be a two-way process. If an organization wants to attract the best employees it is important to sponsor talent, to adopt flexible ways of working, to allow people to take responsibility for the success of the organization. It also needs to be creative, to encourage people to share ideas, to make no assumptions about the way something has to be done but to think about how it could be done differently.

Create an environment where people want to work

Develop coaching, giving and receiving feedback, sharing

Commitment to people development needs to start at the top of an organization; it is not just an issue for HR or learning and development functions. The leadership behaviours set the tone and expectations for employees. People are smart; talented people are even smarter. They will be not be taken in by lip service to values: they want to see an active demonstration in the day-to-day people management of the business.

One of the recent trends in employee development is a recognition that retention of key employees is going to become increasingly important. With reduced resources available, everyone is going to be competing for the same people. Today's younger employees are much more mobile than previous generations.

It's important to encourage managers to be people who make a difference, taking time to 'know' the people they manage as individuals – to cherish, nurture, respect, value each person and watch that person 'grow'. This is the most rewarding aspect of any relationship: to recognize what people are good at, identify their strengths and provide the opportunity for them to use these skills. Empower by communicating, by giving responsibility and the opportunity to be part of decision making. Create a support system to give confidence, stability and security, help people to help themselves. Engender a sense of fun about life and work.

Technology can support flexible working; people no longer need to be in an office. For many people, freedom to operate is important; their creativity is unlikely to be contained within office hours. Allowing them flexibility and freedom will ensure that you maximize their contribution. New legislation related to work/life balance will mean that organizations will have to adopt a more flexible approach.

Working in partnership

The way forward – employees, customers, suppliers, community and the media

No person or organization can function for long alone. Working with people, helping others to be successful, building pride, self-esteem and sharing success are all important components. Equally, building close links with suppliers, encouraging the media with positive news, and building links with your local community, are positive partnership actions.

Brand loyalty is created in many ways, but essentially it is all based on the relationships that an organization builds with its partners. Features like the *Sunday Times* 'Best companies to work for', Investors in People and the National Training Awards in the UK all emphasize the importance of these relationships.

Corporate and social responsibility

Corporate social responsibility is also becoming increasingly important. Organizations are being encouraged to recognize the importance of their role in the community and, through a proactive approach to their corporate and social responsibility, organizations are donating time and products to their local communities as well as money.

No business can afford to ignore its standing in the community or with its customers. One company with perhaps the longest tradition is Whitbread; as Ian Anderson, former Community Investment Director at Whitbread said in *Corporate Fundraising*:

> The provision of financial contributions to the community by business will always be important, but will always be of a limited nature. Donations of gifts in time and gifts in kind can add so much to the fabric of the community and can play to the strengths of commercial organizations by using all their resources.

Communicate the key messages

Internally and externally, gain commitment from others to the key goals

You need everyone to unite behind a common goal. However, you will also need to identify the people who are going to be most proactive. You do not need to call them 'champions', but in reality they will be the sponsors of employer branding. You need them at every level in the business from the very top to the newest recruit. They need to quietly (and sometimes loudly!) promote positive messages about the organization. Those who understand the total impact of the brand need to support others who are less clear, or who adopt a silo approach.

It also means sharing key messages about your business and the opportunities with the people you meet. Questions all organizations should be asking themselves are, 'Are our employees acting as ambassadors for us? Are they talking positively to their families, partners and friends about our organization? What are they saying to our customers?'

Employees experience every day whether you are delivering what you promise and this will be demonstrated through their attitudes and behaviour. Nothing will destroy a reputation faster than an organization promoting itself as an employer of choice only to find its employees informally giving out a very different opinion to its customers, or their own family and friends. People want to work for a company that they respect, and organizations that take employee relations seriously will be seeking to engage the hearts and minds of their employees and seeking to attune their dreams with the organization. This attunement should be demonstrated through the way an organization recruits, develops, rewards and retains individual employees.

From the bottom to the top of the organization (and vice versa) open up channels of communication and encourage the giving and receiving of feedback and, even more important, be seen to be acting on this information.

Sharing with our competitors

Best practice

Be proud of your achievements, and demonstrate best practice. Be the organization that others benchmark against. This will have internal spin-offs for morale. Demonstrating your corporate and social responsibility is one way of addressing this issue. Equally, being part of an employer's forum or network, sharing best practice, being prepared to be involved in the development of shared knowledge, and wanting to create an industry standard are all ways that an organization can input into the corporate marketplace for the benefit of all. If an organization wants to encourage discretionary behaviour on the part of its employees, then it needs to demonstrate its own willingness to support activities designed for the greater good.

Rewarding performance

Real measures that everyone recognizes

Individuals do appreciate recognition for their achievements, being thanked for a particular action. Financial rewards are important, but other forms of recognition are motivational too. Being given extra responsibility, being made to feel part of something special, all are valued by an employee. One concern that people often have is how their contribution will be measured. Measures are not always shared with individuals; the organization may be using one set of criteria, while an individual believes that they are being measured against another set.

This measurement is very much linked to the goal-setting stage. Unfortunately many organizations still have annual appraisal systems that are not linked to the day-to-day activities of an individual. It is important that clear objectives are set, that they are regularly monitored, and that individuals receive feedback and have the opportunity to discuss their own view of their progress. In a coaching environment this will happen more naturally, creating opportunities to regularly recognize achievements, both individually and in the team. Take time to thank people who have met targets, helped others achieve, or gone out of their way to be helpful.

Review and progress

Establish a process to learn and grow

How often do you celebrate success? Be open about measurement and success factors; never forget where you started, and realize how much progress has been made. There should be a process of continuous improvement. Ask, 'What have we learnt? Where can we innovate?' To prevent a distorted view of the organization, the process should be seamless from the front to the back and from the top to the bottom. The most innovative organizations innovate, accelerate and innovate again. The larger the organization the more opportunity there is to learn from different parts of the business. The collective knowledge within an organization is rarely captured effectively. You will find many examples of re-inventing the wheel where there is no effective process of data capture and sharing of best practice or the opportunity to learn from mistakes in a blame-free environment.

Summary – developing people and organizations

Commitment to people development needs to start at the top of an organization; it is not just an issue for HR, or learning and development functions. The leadership behaviours set the tone and expectations for employees. People are smart, talented people are even smarter; they will be not be taken in by lip service to values – they want to see an active demonstration in the day-to-day people management of the business.

Developing an employer brand can help to create a nurturing culture, which enables individuals to give of their best, which in turn supports the organization in delivering its brand promise. As a holistic process it has a dynamic role to play in delivering true competitive edge.

Any HR/OD/L&D/Training strategy and vision needs to be built on the overall business strategy and vision. It should complement the business requirements and be based on key deliverables. Every professional should create channels of influence in order to keep people development on the corporate agenda. The only way that this will be achieved is to become more proactive and to present people development as an important agenda item for the whole business. There needs to be a two-way dialogue and communication and a realistic approach to developing people in the context of business growth.

Take time to explore the content with a trusted colleague from the business who is prepared to give you open and honest feedback. Don't ever make the mistake of hiding away in the HR/OD/L&D/Training department, refining your vision, values and strategy, only to find that when you emerge the key players have made a decision to go and play with the ball in a different part of the park.

Further information on all aspects of employer branding is available at www.employerbrandinstitute.com.

Checklist for developing people and organizations

✔ Examine very critically the current roles and skill sets within your team.

✔ Identify the overall direction of your organization. What are its mission or vision, values and business objectives?

✔ Have standards of performance been set? How are these standards being measured?

✔ How are people being encouraged to develop these standards?

✔ What learning processes are in place?

✔ What are the blockages? What is stopping the organization from developing?

✔ Who are the competitors? What role does their HR/OD/L&D/ Training function perform?

✔ Network with other training professionals. Find out how different organizations are approaching the current business issues.

✔ Meet with the other functions in your organization. Identify what they want from HR/OD/L&D/Training. Put yourself in their shoes. How well are you meeting their needs?

✔ Identify the important measures, for example:
—   speed of response;
—   quality of advice;
—   trainer knowledge;
—   creativity and innovation;
—   will work in partnership;
—   value for money when benchmarked.

✔ Critically evaluate the performance of your HR/OD/L&D/Training.

✔ Set standards and establish an ongoing method of measuring the achievement of standards.

✔ Constantly update within the function, encourage visits, second-ments, and the exchange of information.

✔ Work towards training excellence, to be the organization that acts as a benchmark for others.

✔ Ask yourself and your team, 'How effective are we as a business partner?'

2

Being Professional

The training professional should continually want to develop. Your role is key in the development of other people. Whether you are working with a chief executive officer (CEO) and the board of senior executives, or inducting a new group of employees, the impression that you give to others is very important. You create the brand of training within an organization; whatever training role you have, you can make learning either a very positive or a negative experience.

Developing an understanding of yourself, your strengths, your style of training and your ability to facilitate and coach others is an important part of this personal brand. Only from this understanding can you continue to build your skills and expertise.

We revisit this concept in several other sections of this book as we explore the different dimensions of the HR/OD/L&D/Training professional's role. In this chapter we focus on the underpinning understanding of you.

Being comfortable with yourself

How well do you know yourself? When was the last time you undertook a psychometric test? Can you accurately describe your strengths and areas of development? When did you last undertake any personal coaching or training? It is very easy to neglect our own development – we have all the excuses: no time, too busy developing others, it's too expensive, etc. The real professional, however, recognizes the importance of having a personal development plan.

Where do you start?

In our experience, the better you understand yourself the better able you are to help others. We use the phrase 'being comfortable with yourself' to describe the inner confidence that comes from knowing your strengths and areas of development. We can build a picture of ourselves through a variety of means, but the model of the training professional below illustrates the types of analysis that we can undertake to gain a clearer picture of ourselves and, even more important, how others perceive us.

The training professional

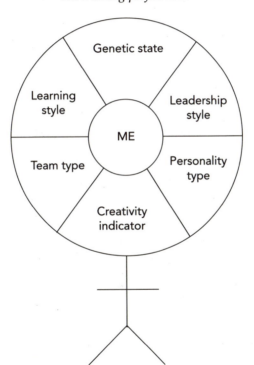

We can enlarge this picture by inviting feedback from others. Lifetime learning gives us the opportunity to explore ourselves and we build layers of knowledge as we work with others. There is a whole range of psychometric tests and other inventories and profiles, and new ones are being developed all the time. The important thing is not just to select one type, and not just to do it once. (One of the authors has developed a range of profiles; contact kaye@theinspirationnetwork.co.uk.)

As we mature, we change, finding new responses to situations. Some characteristics are inherent, but as you become more at ease with the ongoing process of self-development, you will discover other possibilities.

As a trainer or coach you can help others with the same process. It is important to mention here that people need to be trained and registered to give feedback and administer many of the tests. However, once the professional feedback has been given, the skilled trainer/facilitator can help people explore how this knowledge affects their day-to-day working life and, importantly, how they interact with others in groups.

Why psychometric tests?

Psychometric testing is loved by many and questioned by others. The best approach is to be curious – by undertaking psychometric tests and receiving skilled feedback you are building up a picture of yourself similar to the model on page 11. Why we suggest undertaking a range of profiles is that, as in any piece of research, you will identify trends.

Some psychometric tests now incorporate features of others, so that by taking one you may in fact receive feedback about other dimensions of your personality. This is normally indicated in the information about the test. Our diagram illustrates some of the areas that are explored by search agencies and employers for recruitment purposes. However, we also suggest that you explore other areas, such as creativity and learning styles.

The purpose of the tests is to give you enhanced understanding of yourself, but, as with any form of feedback, you should review it carefully and test it against your experience of working with others and feedback you have received elsewhere.

Inviting feedback

Who gives you feedback? Do you invite it? Do you believe it? As professionals we should be able to ask for and absorb feedback into our ongoing development. Unfortunately too few people are really skilled at giving it. If you are training people to assess or coach, you will recognize the importance of doing it properly, but so many people give feedback in a way that is unhelpful during appraisals or performance management sessions.

If you do develop a clear understanding of your strengths, you are better able to help people to give you feedback. By asking the right questions, you will be able to elicit information about your effectiveness as a trainer. You will also, if you are an experienced communicator, be able to identify other people's responses to you. We mention several times in this book the importance of having a trusted colleague who can give you constructive feedback. This may be a line manager, a co-tutor or another team member; the value of feedback from someone you respect cannot be overestimated.

The performance

As a training professional it is important to recognize that people expect you to be able to present and facilitate with style. In running train-the-trainer programmes we encourage people to think about their performance (see Chapter 5, p. 72). With an enhanced understanding of yourself you will find that you are better able to protect yourself from the stresses and strains of being a trainer.

Like actors, most trainers feel excited before some events. This can help you find the adrenaline and energy to run highly participative activities, but it is important to recognize the effect this may have on your body (we discuss this in more detail on p. 15). If you are regularly giving of yourself, you need to find ways of recharging your batteries and keeping yourself physically fit.

Guidelines for a winning performance

Step 1

Create a presence; who am I? Psychometric testing, reviewing the profiles. Talk to people; gain feedback from peers, your boss, family, mentors and friends.

Outcome: An accurate assessment of yourself, your strengths and areas of development.

Step 2

What do I want to achieve? What does the company need me to do? Goals, aspirations, job role, outcomes from business expectations.

Outcome: Clear objectives, a route map.

Step 3

Building the brand, being comfortable with yourself, the presentation, what to say, what to do, what to take, what to leave, what to wear.

Outcome: Creating presence.

Step 4

The performance putting it into practice, first to role-play, then the real performance and then the feedback.

Outcome: The winning performance.

Preventing burn-out

HR/OD/L&D/Training professionals, like other creative, artistic and busy professional people, are potentially susceptible to 'burn-out'. Prevention is better than cure and all the measures mentioned in 'Recharging the batteries' are relevant (see p. 16). Equally with experience you are better able to balance the pressures in your life. There are specific actions that you can take to minimize the risk; see the box below.

Checklist for preventing burn-out

✔ *Get to know yourself. Find out how much sleep you need on a regular basis and try to achieve that amount as much as possible.*

✔ *Eat properly. Find a diet that gives you the proper balance of foods for your lifestyle.*

✔ *Take some form of exercise. Choose something you can do regularly and that gives you an opportunity to meet other people.*

✔ *Develop a support network. Particularly important are colleagues and friends who motivate and inspire you, or who make you laugh, humour being a great stress reliever.*

✔ *Regularly undertake professional development. Identify new skills or areas of expertise you can explore.*

✔ *Each day create space, however little, just for yourself. Whatever other work or domestic pressures exist, devote time to yourself. Use it to do something relaxing, such as reading a book, listening to music, telephoning someone, clearing something off your personal action list or just staring into space.*

✔ *Recognize your achievement. It's wonderful when other people give you positive feedback, but reviewing your own progress can be equally positive, particularly if you have logged your starting point.*

✔ *Be alert to the signs that the pressure is too much. Look for the signs beforehand and do something before you develop the symptoms of stress.*

✔ *Build variety into your working life. Try not to fall into a routine of doing the same things on the same days.*

✔ *Set yourself lifetime goals and regularly review progress against them.*

Handling pressure

Trainers, like anyone else, need to recognize the difference between stress and pressure. We can withstand a considerable amount of pressure, but the physiological changes that occur with stress can be debilitating, which is why the following section on recharging the batteries is so important.

Pressure for trainers takes many forms, depending on their role. For the self-employed independent trainer there is the ongoing pressure of diary management. In this business it is often either feast or famine: suddenly all your clients want you on 15 October, or alternatively no one wants you in July. All the time management and priority techniques in the world will not help you deal with these particular quirks of fate. You can, however, use your knowledge of the training business to protect yourself against these surges in demand. For instance, try to identify the likely requirements of your established clients during the more popular months of the year and, where over-subscription appears likely, negotiate with each of them, trying to meet individual demands as closely as possible.

As in any business, HR/OD/L&D/Training professionals should aim to work in partnership with their clients, and alerting clients about the popularity of particular months in the year is part of that process. During the less popular months, identify design work, or other projects that require less direct training contact.

The need to win business can also create tension, as this is a critically important aspect of business life. But being physically and mentally relaxed and feeling positive often help in successfully winning business.

Time management and prioritizing

Like any working professional, trainers need to plan and prioritize their work schedules. Making time for marketing or administration can often be difficult. It takes discipline to maintain a balanced schedule of direct delivery, design, marketing and administration. You also need to plan breaks to ensure peak performance. These breaks can take any form, but should provide you with the opportunity to focus on something completely different from your normal routine, such as sport, leisure or meeting friends.

Protecting thinking time is even harder, particularly when other people have access to your diaries. In offices with electronic networking it becomes even more important to protect your time. Very few people actually enter into their diaries 'thinking time', because there is a general fear of the comments that such an entry might generate. Many open plan offices preclude the opportunity to think creatively, and people often find it difficult to say assertively, 'I'm going to the leisure centre to think.' However, increasingly, more organizations are recognizing the importance of innovation and creativity and are encouraging a more positive approach to people's needs for space and thinking time.

The need to produce imaginative and creative development programmes can produce considerable pressure, because very few of us can be creative and innovative to order. If your role involves the design of development programmes or the creation of materials, it is important to find somewhere to work that is congenial.

Some of the more progressive training organizations create design rooms for their trainers equipped with flipcharts, lots of wall space, previous course material and other sources of inspiration. For HR/OD/L&D/Training professionals working from home, the same principle applies. You need to be able to create a space that is comfortable as well as functional, and is surrounded by sights and sounds that help you to be creative. (For further guidance on generating ideas and being creative, see Chapter 6.)

Increasingly organizations are recognizing the importance of helping their employees achieve balance in their lives. If you are coaching individuals about their work, encourage them to adopt a more holistic approach, and apply this approach to your own work/life balance too.

Recharging the batteries

HR/OD/L&D/Training professionals are expected to inspire others, but how can you inspire yourself? You need creative triggers (people, places) that you can use to recharge batteries and energize your thoughts, and it is important, because of the nature of your work, that you are able to recharge regularly and efficiently. And you need to identify the triggers and use them before you become depleted.

When we are running management development programmes, we talk about the need for everyone to visualize a place that is important to them, or a time when they were particularly successful. We want people to smile when they think of the image, and we encourage people to go to it regularly to reinforce positive messages about themselves and what they can achieve. The process can help you to relax, or it can energize you.

Music can have a similar effect; some trainers play it in the background during coffee/lunch breaks. Alternatively, it can be used during sessions to evoke memories and to encourage creativity, or as motivational entrance or exit music at large conferences. There are endless possibilities, but in every case the appropriateness of its use has to be assessed against the target audience.

On a personal level you can use music to energize you or help you relax. Many trainers have a selection for different occasions, such as rousing music to help them prepare for their performance, and more restful music to help them relax afterwards. You can create compilations to suit your mood and requirements. If you enjoy music, it can be a very effective method of re-energizing yourself.

Handling difficult people

Most of us have to deal with difficult people at some time in our career. Knowing ourselves can help us handle others in potentially difficult situations. So much conflict is caused by lack of understanding on both sides. Tensions within companies often arise because people are too busy to talk to each other and to find out the truth behind rumours and hearsay. Much can be achieved by identifying the other person's perspective. Customer-focused organizations are recognizing the importance of viewing issues 'through the eyes of the customer'. In any negotiating situation you need to use an enhanced skill set to identify the issue, explore the options and resolve the conflict. The following checklist may help in handling difficult people.

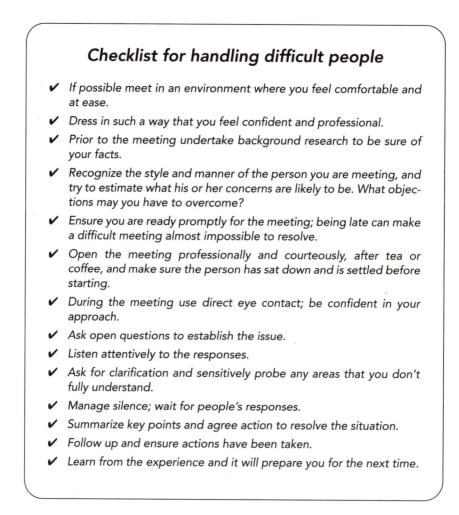

Checklist for handling difficult people

✔ *If possible meet in an environment where you feel comfortable and at ease.*

✔ *Dress in such a way that you feel confident and professional.*

✔ *Prior to the meeting undertake background research to be sure of your facts.*

✔ *Recognize the style and manner of the person you are meeting, and try to estimate what his or her concerns are likely to be. What objections may you have to overcome?*

✔ *Ensure you are ready promptly for the meeting; being late can make a difficult meeting almost impossible to resolve.*

✔ *Open the meeting professionally and courteously, after tea or coffee, and make sure the person has sat down and is settled before starting.*

✔ *During the meeting use direct eye contact; be confident in your approach.*

✔ *Ask open questions to establish the issue.*

✔ *Listen attentively to the responses.*

✔ *Ask for clarification and sensitively probe any areas that you don't fully understand.*

✔ *Manage silence; wait for people's responses.*

✔ *Summarize key points and agree action to resolve the situation.*

✔ *Follow up and ensure actions have been taken.*

✔ *Learn from the experience and it will prepare you for the next time.*

In today's training environment the training professional has an important role to play, and the better you understand yourself, your strengths and areas of development, the better able you will be to help organizations and individuals fulfil their real potential.

Being a thought leader

To be a thought leader you need to express thinking that is original and different. It requires maturity, confidence and self-belief, which will establish your reputation as having something of value to say. To be a thought leader you need to be excited and energized by leading the field.

You do not necessarily have to come up with the original thought, but you do need to be able to grasp an idea and run with it.

One of the really interesting areas is original thought, which is often much harder to achieve. One of the reasons for this is that we often do not create the right environment for originality, or quite believe that we are capable of original thought. Like our intuition, or 'gut' reaction, original thought can be perceived as being a bit 'scary'. We may find ourselves with what we believe is an original thought and then we may be anxious because we have limited experience of being original.

If you do believe that it is an original thought, or a development of an original thought, you need to read about or around it in some depth, become absorbed in it and allow yourself the space to explore it fully. In today's world of global communications there are excellent opportunities for you to share your views, knowledge and expertise.

Always be careful with your intellectual property; it has a value. What is important is that you share the right thoughts at the right time, because if sometimes we share our half-formed thoughts too soon, other people can put a negative influence on us and dampen our enthusiasm. However, we often need a sounding board, someone that we can trust, to share our first embryonic ideas. As part of your support network identify people who can give you balanced feedback, who will help you explore your hopes, dreams and aspirations. If you take your thinking seriously, others will equally begin to develop respect for your knowledge.

So how do you develop thought leadership?

In Chapters 3 and 6 we explore some of the underpinning principles of creative thinking. Here are some key actions for idea generation:

- Take time out to broaden your horizons.
- Be hungry for information, be curious.
- Give your mind freedom to explore.
- Take the opportunity to brainstorm with others.
- Use creative techniques, mind-mapping, blue-sky thinking to push the boundaries of your mind.
- Share ideas with others; use 'displayed thinking' to incubate ideas.
- Practise lateral thinking.
- Build teams of people with different styles of thinking.
- Assess the marketplace, look for the originators. What do they do differently from your organization?

- Do not cling to the past. Spot new trends become an 'early adopter' of new ways of working.
- Recognize that not all ideas need to be new; do not 'reinvent the wheel'; take time to recognize what works well; be prepared to build on the ideas of others to create something new.
- Make sure that ideas are not prematurely shut down; make a habit of asking how we could do it differently. Invite and listen to the ideas of younger employees who may challenge the status quo.
- Be prepared to champion an idea that you passionately believe in.
- Don't just have a good idea: follow it through to a commercial solution.

Creative people enjoy thinking. Often used to spending time on their own, they can be more introverted than others, and sometimes drift off into their thoughts for long periods of time. However, others find that they have less and less time for thinking. When did you last indulge in some thinking time? We don't mean the anxious trying to remember lists of information type of thinking, but real quality reflective thoughtful time, when you immersed yourself in thought so deeply that you had to almost physically drag yourself back to the present.

Following a sequence, exploring options and allowing incubation time are important parts of the creative process. Creative thinking time is a very precious commodity: allowing yourself time each day to explore ideas and new projects is critical to organizational and personal growth. Taking time out to think, to coordinate ideas and chains of thought, and to re-order them into coherent actions is something that many of us rarely find time to do.

Above all, have self-belief. Being original is not easy, and you need a level of resilience to keep going with an idea when others may not see its value.

Career progression

Inside the organization

Working in an HR/OD/L&D/Training department will allow you to make many interesting and useful contacts across the organization. The more consultative your approach to training tasks (see the section on the trainer as consultant, p. 175) the wider and higher in the organization will be your experience. You should be able to develop a real insight as to how other functions operate, how they are managed and the level of staff motivation. The broad areas of career development for the HR/OD/L&D/Training professional within an organization are:

- Grow to be a more senior professional through extending your expertise in key areas.
- Grow through taking on other activities including mentoring and coaching.
- Become a senior member of the HR/OD/L&D/Training function by taking on more consultative projects associated with more significant operational business programmes.
- Become a member of the HR/OD/L&D/Training management team.
- Move from one HR/OD/L&D/Training function to an associated one.
- Move to a function where your business expertise and your facilitative, consultative skills will be of use; this could be a customer service function or sales and marketing.
- Be seconded to other parts of the organization where you will develop business skills and knowledge.

The possibilities outside the organization

There are other ways to develop your career when you leave the training function of one organization. You could join a training company. There is also the path into another organization's HR/OD/L&D/Training function, hopefully in a different role or at a higher level. In the UK these positions are advertised in the HR/OD/L&D/Training journals. Senior positions are also carried in the broadsheet newspapers.

Other possibilities

There are other challenging career paths. A trainer's skills and knowledge, especially consultative business skills, are highly transferable. Many roles are open to the trainer in other types of organization, including:

- becoming a business consultant;
- becoming a 'headhunter' seeking specialist trainers and training consultants;
- training to be a salesman or marketer;
- entering the world of publications or e-learning.

The changing role of training and learning and development

One very real issue for HR/OD/L&D/Training professionals, which cannot be avoided, is how these roles will evolve in the future. Many organizations have already cut their training and development departments as a result of implementing a process of shared services, or alternatively outsourcing some of the more transactional activities. In addition the role of line managers has been broadened to take on more on-job training or developing their employees through coaching.

In theory this leaves HR/OD/L&D/Training professionals with the more interesting and intellectually stimulating work; in practice for many this only exposes a greater problem in trying to identify what the business actually wants them to do. Ulrich and Brockbank, in *The HR Value Proposition*, have added to the debate by suggesting the following roles:

- human capital developer;
- strategic partner;
- functional expert;
- employee advocate;
- HR leader.

Each role brings a level of specialism and allows individuals the opportunity to gain new levels of expertise. With the changes enforced by restructuring HR it is important for training, learning, development and HR to define what they will offer in the future. By working in partnership, departments need to identify where they could help the business. Likely areas could be:

- developing the role of a business partner;
- recruitment, working with the business and providers to find the right quality of staff;
- induction, engaging, retaining staff;
- ongoing performance management;
- ongoing succession planning;
- development and assessment centres;
- brokering training, learning and development solutions, including blended learning;
- employee rights, remuneration and benefits, pensions, community investment;
- acting as an internal consultant.

Working as a business partner

If you are invited to be a business partner, this can only really be achieved from a position of engaging with the business properly. One way of doing so is by researching answers to the following questions:

- Do you have a clear overview of the business vision, values, objectives and key performance deliverables?
- Can you accurately describe the current business success of your organization?
- Do you know what issues in the business would keep your CEO awake at night?
- What are the current challenges being faced by your business sector?
- Who are your key competitors?
- If you had an opportunity to meet with the CEO and board of your business, what would you see as the challenges and opportunities in the business that currently impact on people development?
- Have you identified the key 'touch points' where you need to build relationships with the business?
- Have you identified the key people with whom you need to partner?
- Have you matched them with the right people with the right skills and knowledge?
- Have you created a process to map and capture the key requirements from the business and identified the measures of success?
- Have you allocated a budget to manage the process, resource the deliverables and to develop the skills of your HR/OD/L&D/Training team?
- Have you created an overall brand for the function and conveyed this to the business?
- Have you streamlined products and services to match the needs of the business?
- Have you identified how to create greater autonomy in the business to allow HR/OD/L&D/Training departments to become 'time rich' and allow time to focus on the key deliverables?
- Have you considered outsourcing?
- Have you developed a system of performance management that allows for individuals to be recognized for their contribution and rewarded accordingly?
- Have you created a programme of support for those who under-perform in the new environment?

This is quite a significant list of actions, but these are some of the very real challenges being faced by many HR/OD/L&D/Training departments today. As well as helping you to become a more effective business partner, addressing the learning opportunities on this list can help with your own continuing professional development.

What development do you need?

One of the biggest frustrations for any professional is not being taken seriously. If you feel you are a lone voice speaking wisdom, it is even more frustrating if you feel that no one is listening to you. Like any other influencing situation you need to have a strategy, and the first is to identify the reality of your own position.

People who are successful usually have one or more of the following:

- a belief in their own ability;
- personal presence;
- wisdom, knowledge, or a particular expertise;
- the ability to persuade others;
- status that is respected by others;
- a special something that makes others want to believe in them, be with them, or follow them.

Which of the above do you and your team have? Which ones do you want? Which could you develop? Other areas of development could include:

- enabling skills;
- developing thought leadership;
- business awareness;
- self-confidence and self-belief;
- innovation and creativity;
- doing it differently, growing and managing talent;
- self-development.

If you believe in yourself it is much easier to convince others to believe in you. Self-belief comes from within; others can reinforce it, but first you need to plant the seed. Every national sports team develops confidence by encouraging team members to understand their individual strengths.

The team coach works to build personal strength, team cohesion and belief in their ability to win. If you are really going to help others achieve their personal learning goals, you need to believe in your own ability; you need to develop an inner resilience to help you keep going through difficult times. If you believe in the power of positive thought, you are more likely to be able to support others develop their own self-belief.

You do not need to start trying to influence the whole organization: focus on the parts that you can influence. Explore the concept of change, read about it, identify case studies of other organizations, talk to colleagues, and network with other professionals. Knowledge equals power; seek to influence those around you. Have confidence when talking to colleagues or senior managers, based on the knowledge you have gained.

Personal development

Your personal development plan should reflect those activities you will need to undertake to meet your personal objectives. Such a plan may be provided by your current organization, or you may have to design your own. These personal objectives, both short and long term, will include work- and career-focused items together with more individual, personal items. The plan is focused on improving your performance in your current position and preparing you for your future goals.

Sources of information

There are many sources of advice available to you as you go about planning your personal development and your career. It is never too early to start. You should be seeking the advice of your managers, coaches and mentor. Also consider people you know who seem to have planned their way into a successful career. Use them as role models and seek their thoughts about personal and career development. Another view of the opportunities available to trainers can be gained by reading the appropriate pages in the training magazines (see Appendix 2). These magazines regularly include articles about personal development and career progression, aimed specifically at training professionals, and include interviews with training personnel who have managed themselves through successful careers.

Formal development

Academic routes

One of the ways in which a trainer can develop skills and career opportunities is through formal courses aimed at qualifications. These possible qualifications include PhD, MBA and MSc at any one of a host of universities and business schools. You have to decide in what sphere of excellence you should undertake these qualifications. There are possibilities of gaining these qualifications specifically in HR/OD/L&D/Training.

However, you may decide to use this as an opportunity to extend your more general knowledge. You may well choose to embark on a more general business course, perhaps leading to an MBA. This is a massive career step, particularly if all or part of the funding is from your own pocket. Careful analysis of all the possibilities is necessary. Take advantage of every source of information. Discuss the possibilities with mentors, coaches, managers, HR personnel, and with anybody in your network who has previously made the same decisions. The publications aimed at HR/OD/L&D/Training professionals and many of the national newspapers contain details of some of the courses. Each university, college and business school will have a registrar who will have all the information about that institute's courses. Carefully choose the best course of action with respect to your lifetime goals.

Is it an appropriate route?

The majority of people undertake these high-level qualifications through part-time courses, normally involving regular evening classes and the occasional summer school. There is an enormous commitment of time involved, so the decision as to which programme to follow should not be taken lightly. Examining the possible situations is well worthwhile:

- Why do I want to do this?
- What qualifications do I seek to have? Why are they the most appropriate qualifications for me?
- Where and from whom can I get assistance to find out all the possible information?
- Do I know anybody who has made this decision? What information can they give me? What decision criteria did they use? Are they content with the decision they made?
- Can I receive any financial assistance for the fees? Will my current organization help me? If so, on what terms of contract?

- What level of commitment of time will I have to make? How many years should I be planning to devote?
- What skills and knowledge will I need to start the programme? How much time will I have to spend just to be ready to start the programme?

Other possibilities

A trainer may choose to achieve qualifications closer to the world of everyday training by working towards professional or vocational qualifications. These are particularly designed to help you gather evidence of your competence in the workplace. The advantage of this type of continuous professional development is that you can often gather very valid evidence through normal activities as a trainer. As we have mentioned elsewhere, it is a very good discipline to maintain a personal development plan, because this can help you to focus your gathering of evidence and to identify training needs. You will often find there are local centres that offer these qualifications together with assessor and monitoring support. As HR/OD/L&D/Training professionals you may wish to apply to be an accreditation centre able to offer these qualifications in-house, particularly if your line managers are adopting training responsibilities. One such qualification is based on a series of awards designed to support you in your role as a trainer. They are based on national standards set by the awarding body. More details on professional qualification bodies are available in Appendix 2.

Checklist for personal development

✔ What are my lifetime goals?
✔ Is my personal development plan supporting my lifetime goals?
✔ Who are the useful role models for my career?
✔ What advice can I find in addition to that from my manager and my mentor?
✔ Is it worth attending a seminar on career planning? What books are available?
✔ Is there career and personal development advice available within my current organization?
✔ What journals should I be reading to gain a wide view of my potential development?

Developing new skills

Your personal development plan should include an overview of those skills, knowledge and behaviours you need to improve and/or modify. When this is extended into a detailed skill development plan, it will include answers to questions such as:

- What are the likely sources of the new skills, knowledge and styles?
- To what levels do I need to develop these attributes?
- What measures can I use to test my progress?
- What timescales can I place on my development?
- What help can I expect from the organization, my manager or my mentor?
- What other resources or sources of funding should I consider?
- What contingencies are there if a particular course of action becomes too difficult?
- What are the key milestones in the plan, and what do I need to do to ensure these milestones are attained?

Skills analysis – personal training needs analysis

Many HR/OD/L&D/Training professionals are involved in conducting training needs analysis (TNA) for the organization for which they work (see Chapters 4, p. 49). It should not be difficult for trainers to apply many of the rules of the TNA process to their own skills analysis!

Understanding the current situation

The first stage for an individual HR/OD/L&D/Training professional is to examine critically their current set of skills, knowledge and behaviours. They may be assisted in this by the results of performance reviews, psychometric tests and feedback they have received on projects both inside and outside their workplace. You will also find useful information from the personal analysis we discussed earlier in this chapter. Collect all of the available information together. An interesting approach to analysing all the information is as follows:

- On a large sheet of paper or a flipchart select a number of headings such as 'sales', 'business', 'personal relationships'.
- Now start to use the phrase 'I can' and keep writing all the things you can do under each of your chosen headings.

- Do not forget to include transferable technical skills under the appropriate headings. You may have developed your project management skills to a high level. You may have become an expert in computing.

This can be quite a lengthy process. However, it will probably convince you that your current skill set is much broader than you might have initially thought. Discuss your conclusions with your mentor, your manager and your life partner. Check that they all agree with your conclusions about your skill set, your depth of knowledge and your general patterns of behaviour.

The target skill set

The next major stage of the analysis process is to collect together information on the target skills, knowledge and behaviours that you will need to develop in pursuit of your chosen goals. These targets will be established through reference to your goals and objectives. There will be a mass of information, particularly if your goals are not completely defined. To analyse all this information you might consider this approach. Write three column headings: 'Required skills', 'Required knowledge' and 'Appropriate behaviours', then within the columns list the information you have under groupings, such as 'Company needs', 'Personal needs', 'Input from coaches and mentors' and 'Life partner view'.

Another approach, in conjunction with 'I can' as described above, is to undertake an 'I need' review under your chosen headings and use this to identify new areas of skill development.

Bridging the gaps

You are now ready to make plans to fill the gaps between attributes you have and those you need. Carefully list:

- those skills that need to be developed;
- a priority order;
- the likely ways to improve each attribute;
- a realistic timescale for each part of the plan;
- measures that will allow you to test your progress.

Discuss the plan with your manager, coach and mentor. If the whole exercise has been done thoroughly there will be extensive plans to implement and the plan will cover several years. It is most important to conduct reviews regularly. These reviews should include both progress against the plan and reconfirmation of company and personal objectives. In this way you can reassure yourself that the plan is aimed in the correct direction.

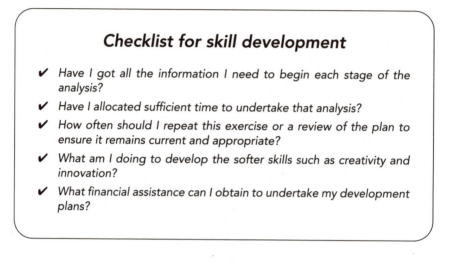

Checklist for skill development

✔ Have I got all the information I need to begin each stage of the analysis?

✔ Have I allocated sufficient time to undertake that analysis?

✔ How often should I repeat this exercise or a review of the plan to ensure it remains current and appropriate?

✔ What am I doing to develop the softer skills such as creativity and innovation?

✔ What financial assistance can I obtain to undertake my development plans?

Membership of professional associations

We have mentioned several times in this chapter the need to have information about news and current trends in your own chosen 'industry' of training. Through their publications, local meetings and conferences the trade and professional associations are the chief source of this information. HR/OD/L&D/Training professionals are recommended to join an association, such as the CIPD (Chartered Institute of Personnel & Development), whose website is given in Appendix 2. Most of the important market sectors also have professional associations and these are well worth joining for their supplies of information.

Joining such professional associations can provide you with more than a supply of news and views about developments in the marketplace. The majority have a range of events which you will have the opportunity of attending and contributing to. This is an excellent way of building your personal network. These organizations, including the CIPD, are often the leaders in setting standards for trainers that are accepted across many organizations. Membership is offered at a number of levels and there are ways of being assessed or taking further qualifications to move to a higher level.

> ## Checklist for professional organizations
>
> ✔ *Do I know the professional organizations in my market sector? Who can I ask about the organization and the value of being a member?*
>
> ✔ *What could I contribute? Could I present at a local meeting? Are there articles I could submit to their journals?*
>
> ✔ *What professional or vocational qualifications do they offer? Are those qualifications appropriate for me now or for my longer-term plan?*

Managing your success

We have discussed the possibilities of developing your skills, broadening your position within your own organization and becoming known in your professional associations. As part of your development plan you should be thinking about marketing your success. This is particularly true as you implement your strategy to progress your career. You are developing a personal brand, and in common with all brands it should be marketed.

Internal activities

You are now involved in self-marketing! Internally you should let your manager and the personnel function understand what you have achieved. You will also have the opportunity of talking to management in functions across the organization. Ensure that they are also aware of those of your skills and knowledge that could be of use to them. Publish successful projects in your organization's internal newsletter. These actions will, at the very least, build the influence of the HR/OD/L&D/Training function throughout the organization. They may result in new personal opportunities.

Be proactive. Use your newly developed skills to plan and promote business initiatives to your HR/OD/L&D/Training management. Ask them if they want you to promote such ideas into the organization.

External activities

Spread your influence externally by offering to become involved in initiatives in your professional associations, the local Chamber of Commerce, local colleges, even with local charitable voluntary organizations. Offer to write papers, to speak at conferences and to do any other things that could promote your name and your abilities.

Checklist for managing your success

✔ *When did I last evaluate my personal brand, my plan for success and my skill development plan?*

✔ *What have I done this month to publicize my success?*

✔ *When did I write, or offer to write, an article for the organization's internal newsletter?*

✔ *What sort of material is most likely to be published in my chosen journals?*

Keeping up to date with developments in training

As a responsible HR/OD/L&D/Training professional you will regard it as important to keep up to date with recent developments in training. Networking is one of the most useful ways to find information about what is happening and about recent trends and issues in learning and development and HR. However, networking is not the only source of such information.

Most of us are bombarded with information about courses, events, books, DVDs, videos, training games and other publications. Online the choice is even greater. If you sign up to membership of various organizations your in-box will be constantly loaded with information. Each and every item is suggested to us by the promoter as being highly relevant. You will need to become an expert in identifying what is important and useful to you rather than just interesting.

With a personal development plan you will already have identified the broad areas of development that are important to you. Having done this you will be able to apply a filter to the information. You will be able to ask yourself if this is important, relevant and helpful to your development. If you actively network, other people will also alert you to those relevant, important events you should investigate. Equally, subscription to one or two relevant training journals will ensure that you are regularly alerted to the latest developments.

Keeping up to date really does require focus, with all this information so readily available. It is possible to spend a lot of time and money unwisely. One key test is will this concept, initiative, process or trend stand the test of time? HR/OD/L&D/Training can be a little like the fashion business in that initiatives have a habit of coming in and going out of favour.

Before embarking on any process of self-development in new areas of training, you should ask yourself the following questions:

- How will this help in my personal development?
- Is it relevant to us as an organization?
- Can I justify spending money on it either to myself or to my organization?
- Will it enhance our offer, or help my organization or me to generate more revenue?
- Does it have credibility?
- Have other people heard of it? Use your network to investigate.
- Are there reputable providers?
- Is it likely still to be relevant in three years' time?

Not all information about trends involves training; we gather much through reading and sharing information through our network. It is important to have reliable sources of data gathering that respond promptly to requests and have up-to-date and relevant information.

Checklist for keeping up to date

- ✔ In what ways will it be easy for me to keep up to date?
- ✔ Will my network regularly supply me with details of new and useful material?
- ✔ What information services are available in my organization or in my professional association?
- ✔ Why do I want to attend/subscribe to this event/publication?
- ✔ What new information will it give me that I cannot get elsewhere?
- ✔ When was the last time this source gave me something of real use?

✔ How quickly could I access data on the latest HR/OD/L&D/Training legislation?

✔ Who can I contact that has the latest information on UK government training programmes?

✔ Where can I find out about external training courses in my chosen development areas?

✔ How much do I use the internet for accessing relevant information?

A note of caution

HR/OD/L&D/Training professionals must have the key skills of recognizing important information, absorbing it and translating the key components into their own work. However, a little knowledge can be dangerous. Make sure you really do understand the concept or approach, and do not be tempted to simply dip in by attending one conference or by reading one or two articles. If you are going to work with people as an expert in your field, make sure that your claim to expertise is valid. There is a real responsibility for HR/OD/L&D/Training professionals to work with people in a positive and caring manner. This development of other people has to be achieved professionally, and you should never train in areas that are beyond your levels of true expertise.

3

Creating a Learning Environment

Many organizations aspire to be learning ones, but it takes dedication to achieve this. It requires commitment from everyone to allow individuals to manage their own development and to support the process through coaching, feedback and ongoing performance management. HR/OD/L&D/Training professionals have a key role to play in the creation of a learning environment; the role may be given different names, such as performance coach, team leader or internal consultant.

The secret to success in creating a learning environment is an understanding of the learning process. Later in this chapter we discuss learning styles and how people learn: it is important to recognize that we all learn differently and have preferred ways of assimilating information. The organization that recognizes this diversity is more likely to be successful in enabling individuals to unlock their potential.

Learning really is a lifetime process, and people working and learning together generate business success. Increasingly organizations are valuing innovation and creativity, but they are not clear about how to create the environment in which people are able to develop them. Some organizations are paralysed by change rather than recognizing it as an opportunity to develop and move forward. At times of rapid change individuals need support to recognize the opportunities this presents, to think laterally, flexibly, and to identify their potential.

The learning organization

There is much talk about creating learning organizations, but less of what this actually means. In this section we attempt to identify what it is and how you can create it.

Our basic premise is that learning takes place everywhere, not just in the classroom. A learning organization has the following characteristics:

- There is a shift of emphasis from trainer to learner ownership.
- The whole range of learning opportunities within an organization is recognized: on-job, off-job, coaching, formal, informal, multimedia, open and blended learning.
- Managers are encouraged to develop coaching, mentoring and assessing skills.
- Additional learning opportunities are created, for example resource centres, learning centres, and continuous learning. Some companies sponsor such personal development, supporting their employees and encouraging them to gain qualifications or to retrain, or encourage creativity by sponsoring product innovation, for example.

Another idea worth considering is that of 'time-out' – one, two, three, six or 12 months' secondment into other industries or education, or doing something completely different to widen people's perspectives and to encourage the sharing of good practice between organizations.

How to create a learning organization

Stage 1

Identify what currently exists: who has received training, what qualifications have been taken, what learning and development structure is already in place within the company. Identify what resources, facilities and budgets are available. Also benchmark: how are other companies organized?

Stage 2

Identify the opportunities within the working environment for coaching, mentoring and on-job training assessment. Match this back to Stage 1; are managers trained to coach, mentor and assess?

Stage 3

Identify pilot potential and a starting point: who is learning what; what are the success criteria, budgetary implications, training requirements?

Stage 4

Create an internal marketing plan: identify how to promote the concept and who to involve.

Stage 5

The process starts. Encourage people to take part; look at the big picture across the organization.

Stage 6

Review the pilot; identify how it matches the success criteria. Promote success, for instance in a newsletter about people's experiences. Ensure there are measures of where it is working, an audit of where learning is taking place.

Importantly, review the process continually. Ask the questions, is it working? Is it working everywhere? How can I as a trainer help the process? What can the organization do to help me help others?

Learning styles

One of the most important factors in the design and delivery of training is understanding how people learn. As a trainer you should recognize and take account of the differences between people's preferred styles of learning.

In the training professional model on page 11 we included 'learning style' as one of the components to measure for your own personal development. It is equally important to help the people you are developing to identify their preferred learning style. By doing this you can help them to recognize what they need to do in a learning situation to maximize their learning.

What are learning styles?

Initial research undertaken by David Kolb identified an experiential learning model that had four phases (see Recommended Reading). He described the first phase as concrete experience, and the second as reflective observation, in which the learner rethinks through what has occurred. The third phase is abstract conceptualization, when the learner makes links with his broader knowledge base. Once this stage has been completed individuals must integrate this new learning into their active experimentation and then develop their own implementation plans.

The experiential learning model

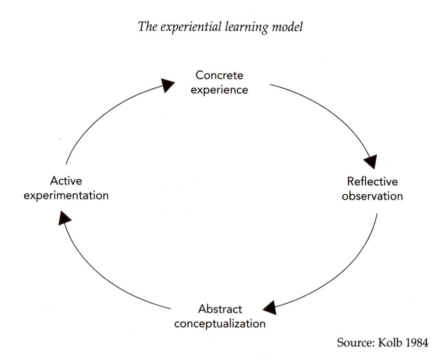

Source: Kolb 1984

This process is cyclical, so that a learner who has absorbed one set of learning experiences is ready to undertake the process again with another learning experience. Kolb's work underpins much of the current research into learning; one example of this is the learning styles questionnaire developed by Peter Honey and Alan Mumford (see Appendix 2 for further information). By undertaking this questionnaire learners identify whether they are:

● activists;
● reflectors;
● theorists;
● pragmatists.

Each style is demonstrated through a series of behaviours and preferred way of learning. For example:

- *Activists* enjoy new experiences and opportunities from which they can learn. They enjoy being involved, are happy to be in the limelight and prefer to be active rather than sitting and listening.
- *Reflectors* prefer to observe, think and assimilate information before starting. They like to review what has happened, what they have learnt. They prefer to reach decisions in their own time and do not like to feel under pressure.
- *Theorists* like to explore methodically; they think problems through in a step-by-step logical way and ask questions. They tend to be detached and analytical. They like to be intellectually stretched and feel uncomfortable with lateral thinking, preferring models and systems.
- *Pragmatists* like practical solutions and want to get on and try things. They dislike too much theory. They like to experiment and search out new ideas that they want to try out. They act quickly and confidently, are very down to earth and respond to problems as a challenge.

By understanding Kolb's experiential learning model you will be able to structure the learning experience to allow the learner to progress through the different stages of:

- concrete experience;
- reflective observation;
- abstract conceptualization;
- active experimentation; and
- maximizing his or her potential to learn.

You can also help the learner to recognize differences between the way they and others learn. In group activities you can illustrate the different styles within the group by asking the members each to work in a way that takes them away from their natural style.

Encouraging learners to find out about themselves is an important part of their personal development. As we discussed in Chapter 2, everyone should have a healthy curiosity about the way they learn and interact with others. Recognizing how they learn, or how they contribute to a team, can be very helpful to the individual learner. A training programme that begins to explore these areas can be a very useful springboard for further development.

Knowing and understanding the implications of learning styles is very helpful in structuring the learning. It has particular relevance if you are working on an individual basis with a learner. It can help you identify the most effective route, through offering on-the-job training, coaching, practical experience or distance learning. It can also be used to help people overcome learning difficulties through helping them to recognize some of the factors that may have inhibited their previous learning.

It is equally important for the trainer to structure any training programme to include a range of activities that will reflect the different learning styles. For example, there should be opportunities for:

● theory input;
● practical experience;
● application of theory;
● ideas generation.

Trainers also need to recognize that their delegates' learning styles may not be the same as theirs. This is where working with a co-tutor can be particularly helpful, as it is likely that your styles will be different.

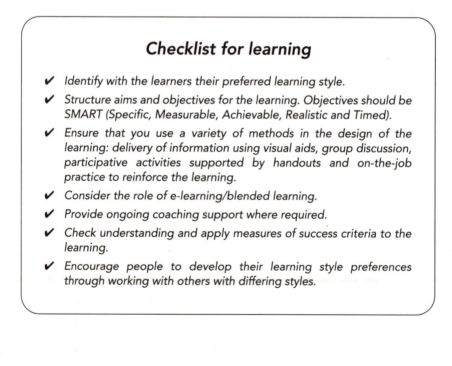

Checklist for learning

✔ Identify with the learners their preferred learning style.
✔ Structure aims and objectives for the learning. Objectives should be SMART (Specific, Measurable, Achievable, Realistic and Timed).
✔ Ensure that you use a variety of methods in the design of the learning: delivery of information using visual aids, group discussion, participative activities supported by handouts and on-the-job practice to reinforce the learning.
✔ Consider the role of e-learning/blended learning.
✔ Provide ongoing coaching support where required.
✔ Check understanding and apply measures of success criteria to the learning.
✔ Encourage people to develop their learning style preferences through working with others with differing styles.

Multiple intelligences

One of the most interesting developments in learning has been the work of Howard Gardner. Searching for an alternative view to the fact that intelligence is a single entity, in *Extraordinary Minds* (1997, see Recommended Reading) Gardner outlined a theory of 'multiple intelligences'. In the context of developing creativity Gardner's work is like presenting developers and learners alike with a key to unlock their understanding about how they learn and how best to learn. Gardner suggests that while we all possess to some degree the full range of intelligences, individuals differ in the particular profiles of strengths and weaknesses that they exhibit. In *Extraordinary Minds*, Gardner suggests:

> These differences make life more interesting, but they also complicate the job of school; if we all have different kinds of minds, then it is simply inappropriate to teach us all as if our minds were simple variations along a solitary bell curve. Indeed each of us should pay scrupulous attention to what is special in our own minds as well as the minds of the children over whom we have responsibility.

The same principle applies to working with adult learners.

Howard Gardner argued that everybody possesses at least seven measurable intelligences, which he defined as follows:

1. *Linguistic intelligence.* The intelligence of words: these people like to read and write, and play word games. They are good at spelling, verbal and written communication. They like learning from books, tapes, lectures and presentations.

2. *Logical-mathematical intelligence.* The intelligence of logic and numbers: these people like experimenting with things in an orderly and controlled way, and organizing tasks into a sequence. They learn by creating and solving problems, and enjoy playing mathematical games.

3. *Musical intelligence.* The intelligence of rhythm, music and lyrics: these people may play musical instruments; they often sing or hum to themselves, and like relaxing to music. They learn by using music, and may use rhymes to help them remember.

4. *Spatial intelligence.* The intelligence of mental pictures and images: these people think and remember in pictures, and like drawing, painting and sculpting. They use symbols, doodles, diagrams and mind-maps to learn.

5. *Bodily-kinaesthetic intelligence.* The intelligence of expression through physical activities: these people are good with their hands. They like

physical activity, sports, games, drama and dancing. They learn through doing, taking action and writing notes, and need frequent breaks when learning.

6. *Interpersonal intelligence.* The intelligence of communicating with others: these are people who are good with others. They know how to organize, relate and tune in to others, and how to put people at ease. They learn from others and like learning in teams, comparing notes, socializing and teaching.

7. *Intrapersonal intelligence.* The intelligence of self-discovery: these people prefer to work alone, and like peace and quiet. They often daydream, are intuitive, keep a diary, plan their time carefully, and are independent. They learn by setting personal goals, taking control of their learning, and reflecting on their experiences.

Gardner also added another intelligence: naturalistic, which is generally taken to mean the intelligence that allows individuals to relate to the natural world and to classify and demonstrate a natural expertise in developing patterns, which can help the individual to develop order from chaos.

Once learners understand their preferences and how they learn, they can use this knowledge to accelerate their learning, and to make their learning experiences more meaningful.

Emotional intelligence

Increasingly both individuals and organizations are recognizing the richness that can also be considered by examining areas that are more personal such as the emotional competence framework identified by Daniel Goleman (1999) in his book *Working with Emotional Intelligence*.

Although it may seem that 'emotional intelligence' is a recent entrant into our vocabulary, it has in fact been acknowledged for a much longer period. Goleman suggests that a number of people have defined emotional intelligence including Howard Gardner (mentioned above), who in 1983 proposed the model of 'multiple intelligence'. Peter Salovey and John Mayer in the 1990s defined emotional intelligence 'in terms of being able to monitor and regulate one's own and other's feelings and to use feelings to guide thought and action'. His own definition includes 'five basic emotional and social competencies':

1. self-awareness;   3. motivation;
2. self-regulation;   4. empathy;
3. motivation;

Goleman's work moves emotional intelligence into the arena of emotional competence, by further defining 25 emotional competencies and explaining that individuals will have a profile of strengths and limits, but that:

> the ingredients for outstanding performance require only that we have strengths in a given number of these competencies, typically at least six or so, and that the strengths be spread across all five areas of emotional intelligence. In other words there are many paths to excellence.

What Goleman and others have done is to introduce the concept of another type of intelligence, suggesting that our skills with people are as important to the organizations that might recruit us as our IQ, our qualifications and our expertise.

Many organizations are also recognizing the impact of this in their retention and development of key workers. These personal competencies together with other traits and characteristics present vital clues to creating meaningful learning experiences.

If the learners you are working with enjoy the learning experience, they are more likely to learn and remember. If they are *told* they need to learn something, their willingness to learn will depend on the respect that they have for the person telling them and their desire to learn. If their desire to learn is driven by a personal curiosity and they learn in a way that reflects their preferred learning style, it is likely that their own enthusiasm and interest will make the learning more meaningful and memorable. To create meaningful learning experiences, HR/OD/L&D/Training professionals and individual learners could do so much more to develop effective learning patterns.

Ironically much pre-school and early years learning does focus on more stimulating ways of learning. Unfortunately, many of the opportunities to really experience learning seem to disappear as individuals progress through school and career.

Neurolinguistic programming

Many organizations have shown interest in NLP (neurolinguistic programming), particularly in the context of personal development and communication. NLP practitioners describe it as an art and a science of personal excellence. It is based on a set of models, skills and techniques for thinking and acting effectively. It was started in the 1970s by John Grinder and Richard Bandler. From their initial work NLP developed in two complementary directions, first as a process to discover patterns of excellence in any field; second as the effective way of thinking and communicating used by outstanding people.

The 'neuro' part of NLP refers to the neurological process of seeing, hearing, feeling, tasting and smelling, ie our senses. The 'linguistic' part refers to the importance of language in both our thought processes and our communication, for example:

- Visual: you think in pictures, you represent ideas, memory and imagination as mental images.

- Auditory: you think in sounds. These sounds could be voices, or noises of common everyday things.

- Feelings: you represent thoughts as feelings that might be internal emotion, or the thought of physical touch. Taste and smell are often included in this category.

People often find that they have a preference in the way that they think and communicate.

'Programming' refers to the way we can program our own thoughts and behaviour, in much the same way a computer is programmed to do specific things. There is not space within this book to explore NLP fully. There are now many books available on the subject, including one that is widely recognized by practitioners as a key source of reference: Joseph O'Connor and John Seymour (1990), *Introducing NLP: Neuro linguistic programming* (see Recommended Reading). There are also courses that will introduce you to NLP in more detail, and can lead to your achievement of practitioner, or master practitioner in NLP.

NLP, as well as building your own skill set, has many applications within organizations, for example in customer service and helping people communicate more effectively.

Knowledge management

Another word that has grown in importance is 'knowledge'. People talk about 'knowledge workers' and 'knowledge management'. What is interesting is that this is not something that is considered as a 'soft skill'. It is about the fundamental point that 'information equals power' and in today's organizations, where a relatively small number of people are developing specialist skills, there is a very high risk of part of the business going with them if these people walk. Today's younger employees are much more mobile than previous generations. In some cases organizations are offering financial incentives to join a company such is the need to attract new talent. Being 'enterprising' is no longer a term just used for people who want to run their own businesses; people need to be enterprising within their own organizations.

Some of the definitions of knowledge management describe how to develop systems to manage knowledge, in the same way as you might want to keep track of intellectual capital. However, the most important factor behind knowledge management is what people keep in their head.

Increasingly people are recognizing the importance of IPR (intellectual property rights). In previous generations individuals who created new learning concepts were only too happy just to have their findings published; now those same findings can also have a value attached to them.

One of the key sources of information about knowledge management is @Brint.com and in an article about knowledge management they include the following:

> Bob Hiebeler, Arthur Andersen's managing director of KnowledgeSpace Intranet (profiled in the 15 May 1998 *CIO* magazine), observed at a recent panel discussion of knowledge management experts: 'to me, this is the essence of knowledge sharing. It's all about contribution, it's all about the respect for others' opinions and views, it's all about a good facilitation and synthesis process, it's all about the distribution of lessons learned from this knowledge process, and it's all about access to packaged knowledge and key insights that become the starting points for individual learning'.

A similar theme is taken up by Brook Manville and Nathaniel Foote in 'Strategy as if knowledge mattered' a thought-provoking *Fast Company* article published in April 1996. They identify the following as key steps:

1. Knowledge-based strategies begin with strategy, not knowledge.
2. Knowledge-based strategies aren't strategies unless you can link them to traditional measures of performance.
3. Executing a knowledge-based strategy is not about managing knowledge; it's about nurturing people with knowledge.
4. Organizations leverage knowledge through networks of people who collaborate – not through networks of technology that interconnect.
5. People networks leverage knowledge through organizational 'pull' rather than centralized information 'push'.

Linking this to a number of case study examples of how this is put into practice, they explain that:

> These successes can be tracked to the superior use of knowledge. And they are much more compelling than the warm and fuzzy argument that companies should adopt knowledge as a philosophical goal since learning and

education are 'good for the company' – or even 'good for society'. The point of a knowledge-based strategy is not to save the world; it's to make money. It's for hard heads.

When exploring the 'pull' rather than 'push' theory, they explain that the power should come from demand rather than supply and that companies run a real risk of overloading their employees with too much information. They also emphasize the importance of on-the-job 'just-in-time' learning, a term that is also used to describe some forms of e-learning (see Chapter 8). They conclude by suggesting that:

> The essence of successful knowledge-based strategies is a company's capacity to raise the aspirations of each employee. These are the people whose contributions and ongoing development become the life-blood of performance gains.

The implication of all this for organizations and HR/OD/L&D/Training professionals is a fundamental shift from training to learning. There is a distinct difference in ownership: individuals need to own and take responsibility for their own learning and it is important to help them realize their potential.

Thinking creatively

An essential skill of a HR/OD/L&D/Training professional is the ability to think creatively and to provide learning opportunities that encourage learners to explore all the potential of their learning style. Many of today's businesses want their employees to be creative and innovative without understanding how such skills are developed (we discuss this further in Chapter 6). In the context of meeting the needs of the learner it is important to recognize the underlying principles of creative thought.

You may have heard the expression 'left brain/right brain'. This concept is attributed to Roger Sperry and Robert Ornstein from the University of California, who showed that each hemisphere of the brain has a preferred way of operating. The left side is far better at performing logical, analytical tasks that require step-by-step logical progression, while the right brain is much better at free-flowing thought, seeing the overview, likes colour, pictures and shapes and sees connections between things.

Sperry and Ornstein's work has inspired a number of present-day people developers to recognize both the differences and the potential for encouraging whole brain activity. Tony Buzan's Mind Maps® concept is an example of this.

The research showed that if you have always primarily used one side of your brain you may find it harder to use the other. Certainly many of us have been conditioned from an early age to believe that we have particular deficiencies, eg, 'I'm no good at maths', or 'I've never been able to draw.' What the work of Buzan and others is showing us is that we need not be totally left-brained, or right-brained; that we can, by using both sides of the brain in our activities, become more 'whole-brained.'

Equally, right- and left-brained people have preferred, or predictable ways of working. Within a training situation the left-brained people will tend to be methodical, neat and tidy, and will complete tasks on time. Right-brained people will use acres of flipchart paper, and it will often be full of images and colour. They may either have not fully understood the task, because they rushed into it too quickly, or their lateral thoughts took them down another track, but they will present it enthusiastically.

These differences are important because, once recognized, they will help learners understand more about how they learn. For example, when you or your delegates complete a learning styles questionnaire (see p. 38), some people may have difficulty in identifying one particular style because their scores may be more widely spread across a number of styles, reflecting both their left- and right-brain preferences. Others may have a high score on one particular style, indicating that they are predominantly left- or right-brained.

It is important that you help people to recognize the potential of whole-brain activity, but you also need to encourage people to respect the differences and to work together, drawing on each other's strengths in particular activities.

These learning preferences also have an impact on the style of the trainer. The left-brained trainer may methodically write down all the steps needed to lead a group through to reach a conclusion, and would be concerned if the group wanted to deviate from that route. The right-brained trainer may have less patience with a group of left-brained learners, who may be taking notes, asking questions or challenging the process.

Co-tutoring can help trainers to appreciate the benefits of the different learning styles, and it can be helpful for groups too because the trainers' combined styles should match the preferred learning styles of the total group.

Within the learning experience there are a number of ways that you can encourage people to think creatively; brainstorming and mind-mapping are just two such methods. Learning can also take place outside the training room: the concept of the learning organization is based upon encouraging learning to take place within the workplace, and individuals being given the opportunity to pursue lifetime learning and to generate ideas for business improvement.

However, one of the constraints on real creative thought is the resistance to the implementation of new and novel ideas. We discuss this further (see the section on the trainer as change agent, Chapter 10), but often really creative ideas founder when someone says, 'It won't work in our organization. Why change? We've always done it this way.'

Trainers need to help delegates not only to explore ideas but also to look at the practical application back in the workplace. In this way the energy and enthusiasm generated by thinking creatively can be channelled positively into action. Creative thinking, together with an understanding of how people learn, is an important underpinning skill for any trainer. For much further support on this subject, see Chapter 6.

4

Designing a Training Programme

Getting started – the initial idea

Depending on your role, you may have full or part responsibility for this, but one of the key skills of a trainer is the ability to design a training or learning programme. At first it may seem daunting, but, like any other task, once you develop a process for doing it, it becomes much easier. The diagram below illustrates the key stages.

Identification of client needs

The normal point for starting the development of a training or learning initiative is identifying the client's needs – what change does the client need in the skills, knowledge and/or attitudes of staff? Clear, precise identification of this need must be completed before any programme design is started. This is the key to the training needs analysis (TNA) or, as is now often called, the learning needs analysis (LNA).

The 'gap' between initial positioning of learners and the required changed position is crystallized into 'training objectives'. Such objectives provide the framework for the training that is to be built and the goals of the training (the goals that are so important to evaluating the eventual success of the training – see Chapter 9), and prompt a discussion with the sponsor of the training to agree exactly what is expected.

To the left-hand side of the 'learning gap' is the initial positioning of the learners before the training begins. This may be identified by observation, by tests or by discussion with learners' managers, or it may be regarded as 'zero' when we assume the learners have no competence in the particular topic before they begin their learning. The right-hand side of the 'learning gap' represents the skills, knowledge and attitudes that the training seeks to develop in the learners. This may be defined by management, possibly featuring as part of the competent learner's job description.

One way of helping a client to focus on their needs is to ask the question, 'At the end of this training, what would you like people to be able to do that they cannot do now, or what would you like to be different?' By asking people to think about the future you begin to identify where to start. Importantly, you and your client should also consider whether training really is the right solution. In today's organizations there are a number of ways, including coaching and blended/e-learning, that may be a more appropriate solution. Another important factor is the duration. One key feature in today's learning is the attention span of learners. Consider really carefully the overall solution and examine ways of proactively involving learners; make as much of the learning as possible personal to them.

Designing training to meet people's needs

As well as identifying the needs of the sponsoring client, you have the individual learner's needs to consider. The very skilled trainer is able to design the learning experience to meet the needs of both the client and the learner.

Designing learning to meet the combined needs is the application of much of the content in this book. In order to design the learning experience, the trainer should have the ability to identify together with the client the strategic overview, the business objectives and the outcomes required from the training. However, once you are in direct contact with the learner(s) you should also be able to respond to their individual needs within the context of the overall desired outcomes.

Often trainers will present the overall aim and objectives and broad details of the content at the start of the training programme or coaching session and then ask the group to identify their specific training needs within the context of the planned learning. In this way you ensure 'buy-in' from the learner, provided you return to pick up the points during the course of the programme. Sometimes what is requested is beyond the scope of the programme, and this needs to be clarified at the time of the feedback, but it should be coupled with a suggested alternative route to meeting those needs.

It is an essential skill of trainers that they put learners at ease and create an atmosphere where people can learn. We shall return to this point (see p. 72). Many of us bear the scars of poor teaching or training, when we were told that we were 'no good' at a particular subject, or we have been humiliated in front of our peers, so the role of the trainer in creating a positive learning environment cannot be over-emphasized. The learner should feel accepted, supported and respected, and that the trainer has a genuine interest in their development.

Some people may have special needs, and these too need to be catered for in the design of training. Specialist support is available for people with learning difficulties (see Appendix 2), but trainers should always ensure that they provide equality of opportunity and are non-discriminatory in their approach to individuals and groups.

Once you understand how people learn you can then come closer to meeting the needs of individuals; this is particularly relevant when working with large groups, or in one-to-one coaching sessions. Use the content from Chapter 8 to explore different ways in which you can structure the learning. With the learners having potentially less time available for off-the-job learning, blended learning may be a more effective solution to meeting individual learning needs.

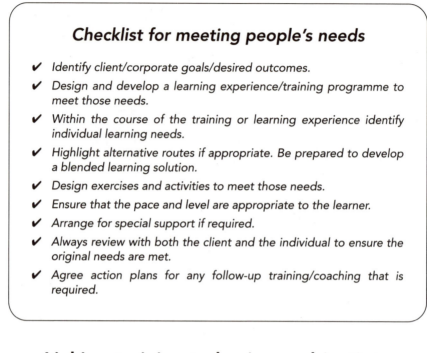

Checklist for meeting people's needs

- ✔ Identify client/corporate goals/desired outcomes.
- ✔ Design and develop a learning experience/training programme to meet those needs.
- ✔ Within the course of the training or learning experience identify individual learning needs.
- ✔ Highlight alternative routes if appropriate. Be prepared to develop a blended learning solution.
- ✔ Design exercises and activities to meet those needs.
- ✔ Ensure that the pace and level are appropriate to the learner.
- ✔ Arrange for special support if required.
- ✔ Always review with both the client and the individual to ensure the original needs are met.
- ✔ Agree action plans for any follow-up training/coaching that is required.

Linking training to business objectives

You may also have to structure aims and objectives, or outcomes, if you are submitting a proposal for funding. To help you identify the outcomes you need to spend time with the client and, ideally, a sample of the learners, identifying their needs. This will help you refine the content and also ensure buy-in from the learners on the programme. This stage should not be too lengthy and should be based on meeting a representative sample of learners and structured around a sample of questions, such as those in the following checklist.

Design of the learning solution

This is the most creative part of the process, the stage when it is important to 'blue-sky' ideas, thoughts and approaches. Tony Buzan has developed a mind-mapping technique that is an excellent way of developing training programmes (see Chapter 6 and Appendix 2). The figure on p. 54 illustrates another model that allows your thoughts to roam as widely as possible, yet still to follow a structure.

Buzan's technique follows a particular process, but you can use the technique in an ordered linear style, or in a more creative way using

Checklist for linking training to business objectives

✔ What are the business objectives?

✔ How will the training help the business to meet those objectives?

✔ What training has already taken place?

✔ What is working well that we can build on?

✔ What needs to be developed, improved?

✔ What new skills/competencies are required?

✔ Who needs to attend?

✔ Who will endorse/sponsor the training?

✔ How will you evaluate/measure the effectiveness of the training?

✔ What information is available about the participants? What do they perceive to be their needs?

colours and illustrations. In this way two people working together on a programme with different learning styles, one more imaginative and enthusiastic and the other more practical and logical, can both use this technique to build a programme. You will see from the model some other important factors to consider at this stage.

Research

Very few trainers are able to create training programmes without some form of research, something to get them started. We have already mentioned talking to learners, but it is also useful to have other sources of inspiration. The more experienced trainers will have built up a resource bank of previous programmes, proposals, content or activities.

Trainers, like teachers and lecturers, are notorious magpies, gathering bright jewels of inspiration. Other people's material often gets recycled under new guises, hopefully acknowledged in the process! However, aspiring trainers should also be capable of generating their own ideas because it can bring tremendous satisfaction. Often these ideas are generated as a result of the background research, or built on from other resources. You can also attend training programmes that give you the opportunity to learn techniques like mind-mapping, or to help you develop your own creativity (see Chapter 6).

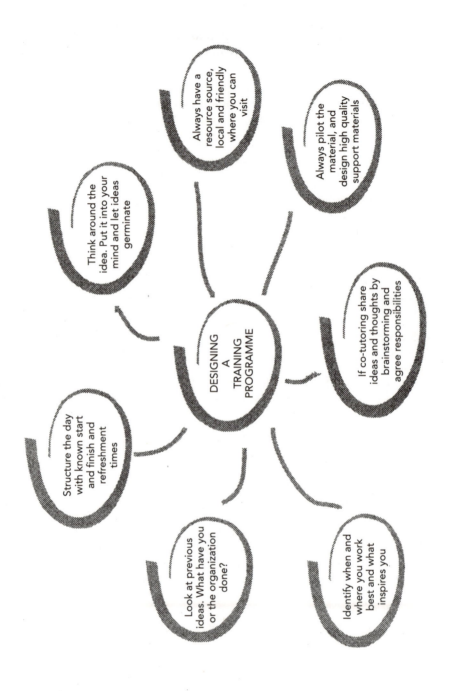

DESIGNING A TRAINING PROGRAMME

Always have a resource source, local and friendly where you can visit

Always pilot the material, and design high quality support materials

Think around the idea. Put it into your mind and let ideas germinate

If co-tutoring share ideas and thoughts by brainstorming and agree responsibilities

Structure the day with known start and finish and refreshment times

Look at previous ideas. What have you or the organization done?

Identify when and where you work best and what inspires you

A good place to start in the actual design of a programme is to work with another, more experienced trainer. It is important to identify the best time and way for you to design training. One technique is to lock the outline concept away in your mind and let ideas about it germinate while you undertake other activities. If you keep a notebook handy, the ideas can be jotted down until you are ready to start the actual design process.

Another technique is to shut yourself away. Ideally this should be in a design room – somewhere with a flipchart and access to pens, paper and other resources so you can apply discipline to the project.

Setting the parameters

After the initial creative stage you need to begin to commit to a framework for delivery. If it is to be a training programme, one way to start is to divide up a page of flipchart paper, putting in the start, finish and refreshment breaks. As a first step this helps you to identify the size of the task. It also helps to make the process more manageable. Then divide the blocks of time into sessions that will later form the basis of your timetable for the day. You may also decide to create headings for the sessions to stimulate interest, eg 'The Art of the Possible', to describe a session on problem solving.

By now you should have identified that it is going to be a training programme. For coaching and facilitation you should also have decided the duration, though this may be revised during the pilot stage. Always aim to design a dynamic, packed programme rather than a stretched event. Sometimes training programmes can be too long and thus lose their impact.

Developing the content

Having identified the time parameters, set about filling the content, remembering pace, variety, attention span and learning styles. (For more information on learning styles see Chapter 3). The key components are as follows.

Introduction

In the introduction you need to set the tone for the event. Ideally, if the programme is internal, arrange for a senior manager to introduce the programme. During a series of events you may need a number of senior people to share this responsibility through a rota system. Their brief should be to set the training into the context of the business objectives, and to illustrate the company's commitment to the training/learning and development.

At this stage you should identify the potential senior people and work up a brief for them, of course allowing them the courtesy of creating their own, though as busy people they may appreciate some ideas from you.

Training/learning objectives

Next you should be able to include aims and objectives. There is a variety of ways that they can be written, but normally an aim describes the overall outcome of the programme, eg:

Aim: To enable area managers to achieve real business success through the effective management of their people.

The objectives are something that learners are able to do at the end of the programme. Objectives should be SMART:

Specific
Measurable
Achievable
Realistic/Relevant
Timed

Always start with a verb, and try to avoid the use of the word 'understand' as it is perceived as too 'soft' and difficult to measure. Use such words as the following:

At the end of the programme the learner will be able to:

describe…
identify…
measure…
consider…
develop…

Beware of setting objectives that are unachievable. Sometimes trainers set over-ambitious objectives that come back to haunt them at the end of the programme. Some trainers prefer to use 'relevant' rather than 'realistic' in the definition of SMART.

Opening session

In planning the first activity it is important to recognize what you are trying to achieve. However well briefed the learner, trainers are often faced with a mixture of emotions when they first meet the group. Therefore, in the design stage, you need to think carefully about the first activity. What are you trying to achieve?

1. *Impact:* You don't want observers or passengers, you want to generate interest and involvement.
2. *Buy-in:* You want the learners, whatever their initial reservations, to have bought into the training, ideally before the first coffee break.
3. *Curiosity and intrigue:* You want them to find out more, to take part in the event.
4. *Energy and rapport:* You want their active participation and willingness to work with you.

With this in mind the first activity needs to help you meet these criteria. It should be quite short and dynamic and may be followed by a short break to allow people to mix with each other. Either during this activity, or after it, you need to provide a vehicle for people to introduce themselves, often described as an 'ice-breaker'.

There are many products that contain ice-breakers; however, if you are not comfortable with the ice-breaker that you select, then do not use it. Almost any task can be used as an ice-breaker if you include an opportunity for people to introduce themselves within the feedback. Also recognize that, if the group already know one another, it may simply be that you need to introduce yourself. Always try to avoid any activity that seems contrived – be as natural as possible. Use a style that is appropriate to the audience.

Expand on the content

In addition to firm, agreed learning objectives, course development should include answering the following:

- Why exactly is the organization doing this? Can I, as an HR/OD/ L&D/Training professional assist any learners who do not know why they have been selected to attend this course, or who are unsure of the organization's reasons for change?
- Who exactly are the learners? Are they fully prepared, briefed and motivated for the training? What is their background, their education, their language skills?
- What exactly do these learners need? Do they require completely new skills, knowledge and attitude or merely a refresher?

- Where will the training occur and what facilities will there be?
- When will the facilities and all the people associated with the training initiative be available?
- How exactly should this change in skills, knowledge and attitude be brought about – for these learners, with these facilities?

Following the first activity, the programme needs to be structured around meeting the objectives. The content should contain a balance of input and participation. The sequence may be as follows:

- input;
- practical activity;
- feedback;
- review of learning points.

Now let us look at each in detail.

Input

Within the initial input you can invite guest speakers, use 35 mm slide, computer-generated or video presentations, or you can present the information yourself. Remember the attention span of your audience and encourage involvement through active participation in discussion or by asking questions of the group. Always provide copies of this information either by printing out copies of your slides with spaces for their notes, or just the copies themselves. Think carefully about when you distribute these. There are advantages in giving them out early as it allows learner a chance to make notes. The disadvantage is they may lose concentration in what you are saying by reading ahead.

Practical activity

The practical activity can be an exercise, a case study, a game/simulation or a role-play. It should encourage the active involvement of all learners. Never provide a task or activity that does not link to an objective, or one in which you have no faith: it won't work! Learners are very shrewd and will reject anything that has no depth.

Designing an activity can take some time, and your sources of inspiration can be varied. It may be based on a tried and tested technique that you have used before, amended to meet the needs of the new group, or it may be something completely new.

You must always research your client group to discover their attitudes, style, energy levels, etc. In your design you should provide relevant examples, case-study or role-play material to which the learner can relate. The material should be meaningful and practical. For example, giving learners the opportunity to work through case studies and to develop solutions based on actual scenarios that they recognize, provides a safe environment for them to test out their ideas and approaches.

A well-structured role-play carefully organized with supportive feedback can provide learners with a real learning opportunity. Equally, business games or simulations can encourage creativity, problem solving and team working. Building up these examples takes time, and once you have established examples use them as models for future exercises. Experiment with a number of formats until you find the one that works best for you and your learners.

Feedback

This needs careful handling – it is worth spending time with the group prior to their undertaking the activity to explain what you expect in their feedback. It will also provide an opportunity for learners to present their findings. They need to be given clear guidelines on the time and quantity expected, ie one or two flipcharts, or feedback to last for approximately 10 minutes. Encourage them to identify someone to present the group's findings.

Review of learning points

Unfortunately this can sometimes be forgotten, or inadequate time is allowed for it. Learners often appreciate the trainer highlighting the key points after an activity. It should not be too long, or repetitious, but take just enough time to reinforce the learning.

Co-tutoring

If you are co-tutoring you need to identify the best way to work together on the actual design – brainstorming, sharing thoughts and ideas about the initial structure and then writing it up separately, each taking responsibility for particular sections. Whichever technique you use, you need to recognize each other's strengths and development areas and divide the work accordingly. (See also Chapter 5.)

The overall programme should be seamless in its structure while benefiting from different styles and approaches.

Action plans

Like the review of learning points, people often run out of steam by the time they reach the action planning stage. Your approach to this will vary depending on the organization. In some cases an organization will have performance management systems, and the outcomes from the course will be linked into their personal development plans.

Others may have a competency framework in place, and the outcomes may support their demonstration of competence. At the most fundamental level you should aim to encourage learners to commit to taking action as a result of being on the course. One way of doing this is to issue Post-it notes and ask each participant to write down one thing that they intend to do differently as a result of coming on the course.

The group then shares their action by sticking the pieces of paper onto a flipchart. These commitments are collated by the trainer and sent back to the learner as part of the follow-up from the programme. This can be enhanced by putting the learners into pairs and encouraging them to exchange telephone numbers and to contact each other in three months to review their actions.

Evaluation

Each programme that you run should be evaluated to provide feedback to you on the effectiveness of the experience, and to provide feedback to your client (see Chapter 9).

Checklist for designing a learning solution

Here are some important points to remember:

✔ *However exciting it may seem in the design stage, any new activity needs to be planned carefully and ideally dry-run through a pilot programme.*

✔ *Never ask participants to do something that you would not be prepared to do yourself. Although trainers are often working to change attitudes, real development does not take place if the participant resents the tutor for exposing him or making him feel uncomfortable in front of his colleagues.*

✔ *Therefore do not create activities or situations that peel layers off people, as it is unlikely that you will have either the time, or possibly* the skill to 'put them back together again'. If someone has a real difficulty, it is often more appropriate to raise awareness, but to follow up with one-to-one coaching or counselling support.

✔ Try to find a local resource centre where you can view videos, games and other activities. This may be a commercial centre or a university/business school library. Membership of professional bodies, such as the Chartered Institute of Personnel Development (CIPD) or the Institute of Directors (IOD) can also give you access to libraries and other sources of material (see Appendix 2 for useful contacts and addresses). Always try to avoid using outdated materials. Look at the date of publication before ordering and always try to view them before using them with a group.

✔ Once you have designed a programme, review it at regular intervals to ensure it is still meeting the needs of the participants and the organization.

Production of materials

This is an important part of the training process, yet it is sometimes neglected. Well-produced, clear information provides a valuable reinforcement of the learning. Technology is evolving all the time, and despite every effort to keep this book up to date new technology will arrive. As a guide, you should use the most appropriate medium for your audience.

What approach should you use?

Your approach will very much depend on your group and the type of event and budget. There are, however, some common guidelines:

● Always produce information that is easy to understand and clear to the learner.

● Use a variety of mediums, eg OHP slides/computer presentations. These should have clear bullet point information or illustrations that make key points. Always check font size for projection.

● Use handouts for the more detailed text, together with pictures and computer screen printouts.

● Use video to provide variety in the delivery of information, but use short inputs, maximum 20 minutes, unless it is used in a trigger format (ie short video input followed by discussion).

- Flipcharts can be used for brainstorming, or outputs from syndicate activities; again prepare where appropriate, write neatly and clearly using dark colours that are easy to read, such as green, blue, purple and black. Avoid red, which is more difficult to read.

How to produce materials

Like many aspects of this book, the production of materials is an enormous area. The breadth and scope of the various methods merit a book in their own right. Our approach is to outline choices and options and to alert you to some of the pitfalls and other areas you should consider when producing materials. However, we also suggest that you seek specialist help in these areas.

Poor materials are actually worse than no materials, so it is very important to plan carefully any material production. The simplest method is to desktop publish hard copy and then to reproduce it using either an in-house photocopier or an external copy shop. You can, if your systems are compatible, take a disk from your computer to a specialist printer for longer print runs or for a more sophisticated design process.

Some people generate their presentation on their computer and then use specialist equipment to provide a presentation to a group or individual. For larger conferences, video, audio or 35 mm slide or computer presentations can be used.

Trainers often focus on learner material but forget their own. Within training organizations, or in-house training functions, more discipline is usually applied because of the need for consistency in the delivery of several courses using a number of trainers.

Even the most intuitive trainers can benefit from having written some notes to define the content of their input. Writing a trainer guide for others to deliver from is an important skill. Writing short notes can help trigger your thoughts and also ensure that you remember key points in your presentation. Again, the production of a trainer's guide will depend on your budget and specific requirements.

If you are working within an organization, or are producing a guide for someone else, the normal corporate presentation for both learners and trainer is a binder of either A4 or A5 format, with two or four rings and tabbed dividers, which guides learners through the various sections of the programme. In writing the content you may wish to adopt the format shown in the diagram on p. 63.

Include copies of computer/OHP slides and handouts numbered for ease of reference within the session tabs.

Trainers have different preferences about giving out the material to

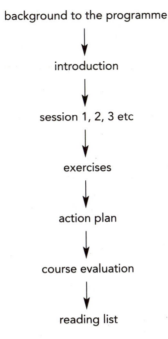

background to the programme

↓

introduction

↓

session 1, 2, 3 etc

↓

exercises

↓

action plan

↓

course evaluation

↓

reading list

learners; some give it out at the start of the course, while others give out session notes as the programme progresses. Some trainers are concerned that the learners will read ahead, or not fully concentrate on the input if they are reading. Usually, if you draw the learners' attention to the guide at the start of the programme and say you would prefer if they did not sit and read it but only refer to it as appropriate, most people will be content to wait. Some people will want to make notes on the guide as they run through the programme.

We have primarily discussed material to support programmes, but there are other types of learning material to consider, eg e-learning and distance-learning packages, management games, multimedia packages, videos, and audio and computer-generated material. Each has special production requirements, and as a rule of thumb, however creative and ambitious you may feel, there is a distinct advantage in producing your first attempts with the help of experts in the different techniques.

The same principles for designing training apply to the design of materials. You should have an aim and objectives, the content should be structured in a sequence and it should engage the interest of the learner. It is possible, in the excitement of working in other media, to forget the basics of good practice, and end up with not very interesting content. Any form of learning support should have a structure and a purpose and should add to the learning experience rather than detracting from it.

Scheduling the production of materials

It is easy not to allow enough time for the production of materials, but it is an important part of the planning process, and once the date for the learning event has been identified, you should work back from that date to identify the production schedule. Whatever is being produced needs to go through several stages, all of which need a timescale attached to them:

- overall aim/objectives set;
- outline content set;
- schedule for production agreed;
- guidelines for format, typeface, font agreed;
- outline first treatment produced;
- client/author's amendments added;
- proofing, final version produced;
- client's approval given for production.

Depending on the involvement of other people, such as the client, the draft stage may involve the production of a number of versions, in which case you repeat the stages of amendments and proofing prior to the final sign-off. Although this may seem a tedious process, by adopting a methodical approach to the final stages you will avoid the expense of re-doing materials because of errors, which can be particularly costly when the material is being produced for a large number of programmes.

Costings

As we highlighted earlier, the potential for escalating costs in the production of materials is a very real threat. For the inexperienced trainer, purchasing from outside providers is fraught with danger. Most corporate organizations have purchasing procedures that help to eliminate some of the problems. Whether you are part of an internal structure or a sole trader there are some important points to remember (see checklist on p. 65).

Designing training can be one of the most satisfying and stimulating tasks for a trainer as you begin to highlight and identify learning opportunities. Always dedicate quality time to the process, and ensure that the final stages of the production of materials are not rushed.

Checklist for producing materials

✔ Obtain a number of written quotes from a variety of sources.

✔ Choose a reputable firm, agree timescales and carefully manage the project.

✔ Always proof and compare the final version with the original.

✔ Be aware that large-scale changes may incur extra costs, particularly in the final stages.

✔ Adhere to corporate identity guidelines where they exist.

✔ Take care not to infringe copyright.

✔ Build in contingency times.

✔ Obtain a sign-off from the client before the production run.

✔ Always carefully inspect the final product.

✔ If there is a long print-run, ensure that you sample a number of the produced materials to ensure that the quality is consistent throughout.

✔ If you are dissatisfied, immediately go back to the producers of the material with your complaint. Ask them to suggest ways of rectifying the problem.

5

Delivering Training

Methods of delivery

Having designed the training it is important to deliver it effectively. If you are regularly delivering training, you will be aware of many of the points that make for effective delivery; however, if you are new to training you should prepare very carefully. No trainer or line manager should attempt to run a formal training session without being trained themselves. Most companies run train-the-trainer programmes for their internal trainers, or there are external providers (see Appendix 2).

Your style of delivery will very much depend on the type of event you are planning. As a trainer you will be performing a number of roles: direct training, one-to-one coaching, facilitating and/or presenting at a conference. (See Chapter 10 for specific input on different roles.) However, as we discussed in Chapter 2, there are important underpinning skills that every trainer needs in order to be successful.

In this section we look at delivering a training programme. If the programme has been carefully designed, your life as a trainer will be much easier. You should be supported with all the material necessary to run the event. There are a number of key stages within the delivery process.

Before the event

Ensure that all participant material is completed and ready for use. Your trainer's guide should be complete with your guidance notes, copies of 35 mm slides, computer-generated presentations, videos and other supporting material.

Take time to run through the content. Some trainers like to make additional notes to support their presentation. Always make sure that these are written large enough to be read at a distance. Start each key area with a new page, or a new card, and always number the pages. Sometimes, if people are delivering a formal presentation, they will use postcards with key points written on them. Again either join them together with a tag or number the cards.

Prepare a box containing all the support material that you may need. Sample contents could be:

- pads, pens, tent cards/name badges for the learners;
- spare flipchart paper: if you are using a hotel check what they are supplying;
- marker pens, Blu-Tack®, masking tape;
- A4 paper for individual and group activities;
- stapler and staples, paperclips, Post-it® notes, scissors, glue, rubber, ruler, pencils, pencil sharpener;
- calculator (sometimes required for group activities involving finance);
- other items specific to group activities, eg rewards, prizes for games; some corporate events include larger gifts for team games;
- promotional material, such as pens, hats, T-shirts, polo shirts and other branded goods, which are sometimes requested at team events; these need to be ordered in good time with sizes checked and agreed prior to the event.

Ensure that the venue has been booked and that a letter with the details of the timetable, start and finish times, refreshment breaks, any special dietary needs and the equipment requirements is sent either to the external venue or to an internal facilities manager.

If you or the learners need overnight accommodation ensure it is booked and confirmation is received. Take time to run through the programme and have prepared any additional notes or comments to support your delivery.

Ensure that you and your learners have a letter with full details of the day's timetable, the venue, maps and directions, any special clothing required (eg if there are leisure activities ensure that people know so that they can bring the correct clothing). Also people should be told if dress is to be casual during the day, or semi-formal in the evening.

Prior to the event you should also decide what you are going to wear so that if anything needs cleaning, or you want to buy something new, everything is organized in plenty of time. Trainers often move from hotel to hotel, in and out of cars, aeroplanes, so investing in easy-care, coordinated outfits makes life much easier. Equally you often need clothes that are defined as 'smart casual'. As a trainer you are often very active, so wear things that look smart and professional but are also comfortable. Some trainers also take a spare shirt/blouse to change into during the day, usually the same colour. Alternatively, they travel in very casual clothes and change once they have set up the room, so they feel fresh at the start of the event.

Always allow plenty of time to travel to the event and have a back-up route planned. Consider staying at the venue the night before if there is a chance that you may not arrive in time, or you will have to get up so early to reach it that you will be tired during the day.

The night before the event work through the programme session by session. You will often find that fresh points occur to you. Make additional notes in your trainer's guide if you feel they are important. Resist massive re-scripting at this stage.

If it is a particularly important event, arrange for a friend, relation or partner to call you to wish you good luck or simply to remind you that there is another world outside!

Finally, relax, do something that you enjoy and go to bed at a reasonable time, having set up an early morning call or alarm and booked a taxi if required, or checked the car for petrol, etc.

Checklist for delegate readiness

The greater the delegates' knowledge of the course, the more quickly the trainer can start the day and the more the delegates will gain from the event.

- ✔ *Distribute useful pre-reading at least two weeks before the event.*
- ✔ *Ensure delegates understand the importance of the course to the organization and to themselves.*
- ✔ *Provide an overview of the programme so that delegates understand what will be covered.*
- ✔ *Ask delegates to consider their needs from the course, to discuss these with their own managers and to bring a list to the course.*
- ✔ *Encourage delegates to 'read around' the topics of the course.*
- ✔ *Whenever possible, provide a list of questions for the delegates to research before the course to focus their preparation.*

On the morning of the event

Arrive with time to set up the room. Normally, the room will already be arranged in the formation you requested, but often some of the finer details may not have been understood. Sometimes the instruction has not been given to the relevant people and there is a degree of furniture moving to be undertaken. Always elicit support if it is available.

Ensure that all the equipment works. Be particularly sure to check television and video connections, and make sure that the television is tuned to the video channel if you are planning to show a video. Put the video in the machine and make sure it is at your starting point. This can save you the embarrassment of trying to show a video to the learners and it not working. Again, in-company technicians or hotel staff can help you.

Most organizations now use computer-generated presentations, but if you are using an OHP, make sure the projector focuses on the text by testing it with an OHP transparency, and make sure the projector glass is clean. Check the angle of projection and also ensure that it is far enough away from the screen to project a clear image. Check from the back of the room, walk around and make sure that there are no blind spots for learners. If you are using a computer-generated presentation, before the event ensure that the font size is large enough for your learners to read easily. Also, check that the background colour is not too dark, or too busy for viewing.

Very few rooms are ideal for training, many being hot and stuffy with poor air-conditioning. Do everything you can to achieve the right working conditions. This may mean resetting the temperature on the air-conditioning, or locating windows and opening them prior to the event. So many training programmes are marred by uncomfortable environments. This underlines the importance of checking the venue beforehand.

Lay out the material for learners, including the learner guide, pads, pens, tent cards and/or name badges. Make it look welcoming and inviting.

It is often easier to prepare your first few flipcharts beforehand. Include an initial message, such as 'Welcome to... [insert title of your programme]'. Write your name on the corner of the page, or on a tent card at the front of the room, or put on a name badge.

Check on the arrangements for the coffee/tea on arrival and that water/fruit juices/squash are on the learners' tables. Where possible arrange for all-day refreshments. This means that you can take shorter but more frequent breaks without having to wait for the arrival of refreshments. Giving learners regular breaks often helps with the learning process.

Find the facilities manager or venue organizer and ensure that they have the latest copy of the programme, and impress on them the importance of the prompt arrival of refreshments.

Check the locations of the fire exits and washroom facilities, and if the event is residential, identify when learners will be able to go to their rooms.

Locate syndicate rooms, dining rooms, photocopier/fax and business centre support, and agree arrangements for payment for these facilities. This saves escalating charges by over-enthusiastic learners. Locate in-house telephones and payphones.

Set out your slides, trainer's guide and other things that you need to run the sessions. You will find it easier if you have a table at the back or side of the room for additional handouts and exercise material. In this way you can keep the space at the front for your slides.

Make a final check that all the equipment works. If it is a formal presentation and you are working with an auto-cue, or someone else is running your slides for you, meet them beforehand and agree a set of signals between you to ensure it all runs smoothly. Remember, if you are given a battery microphone, switch it off when you are not presenting!

Just before you start, allow yourself a few minutes for personal preparation. Walk outside for some fresh air, make a final visit to the cloakroom, check your appearance, relax, breathe deeply and walk back to the room ready to meet the learners.

Checklist for a successful delivery

✔ Once the programme is designed, spend time becoming familiar with it.

✔ Plan a dry run either by yourself or with a co-tutor.

✔ For major programmes run a pilot.

✔ Prepare a checklist to ensure everything is organized at the venue (see the example in Appendix 1).

✔ Make sure your travel and accommodation arrangements have a contingency time built in. Always try to arrange overnight accommodation at the venue the night before your programme if it is far away.

✔ Be careful what you eat and drink the night before. Breathing garlic fumes over the delegates, or suffering from a hangover, is not the best way to start a programme.

✔ Use relaxation techniques or favourite tracks of music to relax or energize yourself prior to the event. Have a tape in the car and play it on your journey.

✔ Just before you start, go quietly outside the room and compose yourself.

The delivery

When you are ready and it is the correct starting time, encourage the learners into the room and welcome them to the event. Always try to start promptly or if you know some learners are delayed, tell the rest of the group and arrange a new start time. It is often better to start and allow latecomers to join the group than keep people hanging around. Ensure you spend time with those who arrive late helping them to catch up with the key information they have missed.

Sometimes you may have a senior person to open the event. Ideally, ask them to do their input first so that you can then run the rest of the programme without interruption. Hopefully they will be motivational and helpful in setting the tone for the day.

At the beginning of your input you need to introduce yourself, list the procedures to be followed in the event of an emergency and give other domestic details like the location of washroom facilities.

Follow this by encouraging people to write their names on tent cards. Do not assume that if they are from one organization they automatically know each other. Even if they do know each other it is quite in order to say, 'It would help me if you could all briefly introduce yourselves and say a little about your experience.' Normally this can be structured by asking for the following:

● name;
● job title;
● years of experience; and
● any previous training attended.

It is important to try to learn the learners' names. If you have a problem remembering names try to find a way of overcoming this. The following points may help:

● As the learners introduce themselves jot down brief details about them in the same formation as the seating. This can also help later in the day when you are dividing them into syndicate groups and you want each group to contain a range of expertise.
● Some people reinforce their recollection of people's names by repeating the names several times in the initial conversation, eg thanking them by name for their contribution.
● Talking to people on a one-to-one basis during the breaks helps to add other pieces of information to their name.

● One well-known ice-breaker is to ask people to give the usual information and then to tell the group something unusual about themselves that no one else knows, eg, 'My name is George and I breed green canaries.' It's a test of everyone's memory to repeat this later and to identify what the group can remember about these initial introductions.

In running the first session, give learners the opportunity to settle and to start participating. If the programme has been well designed there will be a good balance between input and activities. (The development of the content was covered in detail in Chapter 4.)

Your style

However well the programme has been designed it is the trainer(s) who bring it to life. As we discussed earlier, your role is critical to the success of the event.

You should encourage interaction, manage questions and help everyone to contribute and feel part of the event. While debate is an important part of the learning, you also have to oversee it to ensure that one or two learners do not control all of the discussion, leaving the rest of the group as observers.

The experienced trainer develops the ability to answer the questions, widen the debate to include others as appropriate and then to move on. If your programme has been carefully timetabled, you will lose valuable time if you do not control the event, and then you lose respect from your group. Always acknowledge a good question and try to respond positively, even if it is a sensitive area. If you do not know the answer, or the questioner appears to want to monopolize the session, suggest that you discuss it with them later on a one-to-one basis.

Sometimes you may have to handle conflict, or facilitate the group to handle difficult situations. Always be sensitive. Recognize individual learning styles (see Chapter 3) and the differing needs and experience of individuals.

During the event you should be ultra-observant, ensuring that the group stays with you and recognizing when someone is struggling or feeling uncomfortable. Take time during the breaks to get to know the person, and try to encourage them to articulate their concerns so that you can help them to overcome the issue, either during the programme or after the event, perhaps through coaching. It is not appropriate to discuss potentially sensitive areas in front of an individual's peers, and you need to respect their need for privacy.

As a trainer you are in powerful position. Never abuse it. Instead, use your skill to work with all the members of the group while recognizing the different individual starting points.

The more relaxed you are, the better you will be able to work with the group. If you are co-tutoring you must establish a way of working that lets you both use your individual strengths to facilitate the progress of the event (see the section on co-tutoring, p. 77).

The pace of the day should be carefully controlled to allow for maximum participation from the learners. It is important not to have too much input from the trainer at any one time; instead structure these slots throughout the day. Carefully watch your group for signs of boredom, discomfort or loss of involvement.

You also need to manage your own energy levels, as running training events can be exhausting. Eat and drink sensibly during the day to ensure a balanced sugar level. Sometimes trainers find themselves running out of energy or getting 'hyper' because they have eaten the wrong food or drunk too much coffee during the day. Five light snacks may be best for you, using fruit where possible. This is also important for learners. Try to avoid the provision of heavy lunches and encourage them to get some fresh air, which will help them to maintain concentration. (This does not mean a visit to the nearest pub!)

If you have time, also take a break outside; it will help to clear your head from the morning's events. Use the time to review the progress of the group, either by yourself or with your co-tutor.

Always plan a practical activity for after lunch, traditionally known as the 'graveyard slot', because learners often find it hard to concentrate at this time.

Keep checking the temperature in the room during the day. Sometimes there is a build-up of heat as the day progresses, which results in the learners feeling lethargic.

You should also be assessing what progress is being made against the objectives. Are you achieving what was hoped for? Do you have any outstanding learner requests that have to be met? Are you running to time? Do you need to amend any of the content? Have you encouraged the learners to mix with each other through different pairings or syndicate work? Always be flexible, but stay in control of the overall process.

As the day reaches its conclusion you should either be summarizing and encouraging the group to identify their action plans, or setting up evening activities, or plans for the next day if it is a longer programme.

Checklist for delegate involvement

The more involved the learners, the more they will learn and remember.

✔ Regard your role as a facilitator of learning rather than a deliverer of information; your role is helping the delegates to learn themselves.

✔ Even for those with a more theoretical learning style, the ancient Chinese proverb holds true: I hear: I forget. I see: I understand. I do: I learn.

✔ Encourage the learners to talk and do so as early as possible through ice-breakers and through discussion of expectations and needs from the workshop.

✔ Use open questions to the group to inspire conversation.

✔ When delegates ask interesting questions, use those questions as discussion points by sharing them with all the delegates.

✔ Show your interest and enthusiasm for the topic and for developing new learning, otherwise you cannot expect the delegates to be motivated.

✔ Make practical sessions as relevant as possible to the delegates' own roles.

✔ Regularly take feedback from another trainer; use a camcorder to record your own performance; make sure you are not too domineering.

✔ Prepare, plan and practise to ensure you will deliver with confidence and to allow yourself to focus on the delegates' needs.

✔ 'Chunk' the learning material so that you change the focus and the pace often.

✔ Secure the learning of each topic before moving forward; assess the delegate's capabilities and summarize the topic before going on.

✔ Introduce each topic succinctly; abruptly moving to a new topic can disturb delegates.

✔ Encourage all delegates to prepare an action plan, take it back to their managers and discuss what they have learnt, its significance to the learner's own needs and how the learners intend to use their new capabilities.

Residential events

Sometimes training events run for a number of days, but the same delivery principles apply as to short events. However, you do have to manage the learning process even more carefully. Residential events are more exhausting for everyone. The trainers often feel that they are never off duty, and the learners often feel the peer pressure of not being the first to go to bed!

A balance must be set, with clear guidelines established at the start of the event. Residential programmes are an expensive investment and learners need to recognize that the prime purpose is to help them develop new skills rather than an expenses-paid holiday. Heavy drinking into the early hours often has a negative effect on their ability to absorb any information the next day. Senior managers can often help the trainers in setting the scene and emphasizing the company's commitment to personal development. Equally, some companies reward their teams by organizing residential events, and so activities should have sensible end-times to allow people to relax and socialize and switch off from the day's learning.

Ending the event

Whether it has been a one-day programme or a longer event, the key outcome should be that the learners are able to go back and *do*. If the objectives have been achieved, then the learners should be setting action plans ready to review them with their line managers.

Every training event should have a significant impact on the individual and the business. You want learners to leave feeling positive and motivated and not just on an adrenalin 'high'.

You should always allow enough time at the end of the programme for both the action planning and the evaluation (we cover evaluation in depth in Chapter 9). Most trainers also finish with some opportunity for the learners to comment on their own personal learning experiences during the event.

Always thank the learners for their attendance, and ensure that you did meet the objectives and their needs. Highlight any follow-up training that has been organized, and offer a contact number for any individual follow-up needs.

After the learners have left, gather together all the materials and put them into the right order ready for filing or to be used again at another event. Check the syndicate rooms for any resources left behind. If you are writing a post-course report, remember to save any relevant flipcharts or other materials.

As you are leaving the venue, remember to thank the catering and facilities staff for their help. Also make a note of any difficulties that may have occurred to ensure that they do not happen again if you revisit the venue.

Finally, go home, relax and positively switch off!

Reviewing the training

It is important to set a time when you will review the event. This may be with your co-tutor, but should also involve the client. Normally, this is planned before the training, but always try to ensure that it happens. A review of every event is a key part of the overall evaluation of a training programme.

Prior to this meeting, while the event is still fresh in your mind, make brief notes of the learning and action points. You may have identified further training needs with members of the group, or you may have identified follow-up business actions. You may well have identified items for your own continuous professional development (CPD) in pursuit of improving the effectiveness of your training.

Your review will be assisted by the 'course assessment' forms completed by the learners at the end of the course. In Chapter 9, we refer to a checklist for reviewing other trainers' training delivery (see Appendix 1). Use this either to review your own input, or with your co-tutor. Ask yourself these questions:

- What did I do to involve the learners?
- Which parts of the programme really worked?
- What parts need improving?
- How well did we work together as a training team?
- What would I/we do differently next time?

Checklist for good presentations

The following checklist is designed to highlight some key points in giving a presentation or delivering a training programme.

✔ *Most presentations are computer-generated but if you use OHPs, reveal transparencies by using a piece of paper under rather than on top of the transparency (this prevents the paper falling off).*

✔ Do not read from the slides as this insults the intelligence of your group. Make key points instead.

✔ Use a pen to highlight points by laying it on the overhead projector itself rather than prodding the screen (choose one that does not roll).

✔ Use laser beams or pointers only if you are comfortable with them. (Nothing is worse than an out-of-control laser or pointer.)

✔ If you are using 35 mm slides or a computer-generated presentation ensure you are totally in control of the equipment. Check and double-check!

✔ The same principle applies to video equipment of any sort. Practise beforehand with the equipment to ensure that it all works.

✔ If in a strange venue, make arrangements for someone technical to be on hand to help you if there is a problem with equipment. Always check there are spare bulbs, etc.

✔ Recognize that some time in your career it may all fail and you will have to cope by using other means to illustrate your points.

✔ When using flipcharts try to have as much prepared as possible, and write clearly and in straight lines (some flipcharts come with feint lines or grids). Try to have perforated flipchart paper for ease of tearing off sheets.

✔ Avoid the use of orange and red on flipcharts and OHP slides as they are difficult to read from a distance. Dark blue and green are ideal alternatives to black.

✔ Water-based board marker pens are kinder to the atmosphere than spirit-based pens, particularly in smaller training rooms.

As well as delivering training, trainers sometimes have other responsibilities, or need to work in different ways. The next sections deal with some of these aspects.

Co-tutoring

If you are working as a team you need to agree how you are going to work together. There are real bonuses in working as a team, particularly if you have different styles, as it provides variety for the learners and also helps you retain a freshness. The trainer not delivering can be observing the group and can give valuable feedback to their partner on the responses from the group.

It is important for people working together to agree styles and approaches and to give each other feedback on how the relationship is working. It is worth spending time on this because a good delivery team not only benefits the learners but can be a tremendous source of feedback and personal growth as the trainers learn from each other.

Sometimes you co-tutor with a client or a line manager. This too may need careful handling and agreement of roles and responsibilities, particularly if the client is less experienced than you. A client will not thank you for making them look or feel small in front of their colleagues. Planning the inputs carefully and having a dry run can help the situation.

With experience and careful feedback you will identify people with whom you can work. You should set the ground rules so that you have a clear understanding of how you will work together. Healthy debate is positive, but learners do not want to witness trainers competing with each other, or to be confused when they argue or give conflicting views.

Equally important is agreeing how to add supplementary information. Sometimes the other trainer wishes to contribute to the discussion, which should be done at an appropriate moment by giving an agreed signal to the trainer who is delivering, who can then bring the co-tutor into the conversation.

This technique can also be used very effectively to support a trainer who may be experiencing difficulties with a group. The co-tutor should never take over, only make her point and then hand back to the main tutor. It is worth continually giving each other feedback on the workings of the relationship, because when it works well a training partnership can really inspire a group.

Train-the-trainer

As you progress through your career, there will be times when you need to develop new levels of expertise. One way of doing this is to be trained. When trainers are being trained in a new area this is normally called 'train-the-trainer'. In its purest sense the training may be designed for people who are already trained in the techniques of training but who wish to develop new areas of expertise.

In these cases you are normally given a trainer's guide and trained in the content of the specific new area. If it is part of a much bigger roll-out programme, you will normally not be allowed to run the programme until you have been trained and had practice runs at delivering the material.

Equally, you may attend a train-the-trainer programme to help you develop the basic skills of training; once you have attended this you should have the opportunity to practise with extra top-up sessions as required.

Developing as a trainer is a lifetime process, and it is likely that you will attend many such events during your career.

Other training communities

Trainers are not only to be found in human resources and training/ learning and development functions. Across many organizations there are individuals who spend much, if not all, of their time in training-related activities, including the facilitation of courses and of one-to-one coaching. These situations are discussed in detail by Mackey and Livsey, (2006) in *Transforming Training* (see Recommended Reading).

It is not unusual for specific functions to have their own trainers. Sales training is traditionally facilitated in many companies by internal trainers who report directly to the sales function and not human resources/ training and development as well as by external facilitators. As central training functions decrease in size, other functions take on responsibility for their 'own' training of staff. Another, massively increasing, community of trainers is associated with information systems – particularly 'help desk' personnel, who spend much of their time training users on systems, sometimes in an unstructured manner in response to a fault call, sometimes in a structured manner when several users are called together to be trained on a new system. Often a number of users of a system are themselves trained as the first, 'super' users with an agreed role to assist others as the system is taken up.

Sales trainers

Training sales people, often highly personally motivated, short of time and short in attention span, is a highly challenging activity! The trainer needs to provide high-activity training that shows continuing high levels of benefit for the learners – otherwise the temptation of their e-mails becomes too much! The nature of sales people demands that they need to have respect for the trainer, who needs to show a deep understanding of his learners' lives and their motivation – most usually by having a first-rate sales 'track record' himself. Anecdotes, tricks and new techniques quickly acquired are often the order of the day on a 'skills-based' sales workshop. Sales people will, given an understanding of the inherent personal benefits involved, be prepared to deeply absorb themselves in case study-based activities – particularly if these case studies feel 'real' and 'customers' are role-played by authentic people. Sales people often do not have the same reluctance for role-plays shown by other staff – even with video recording!

IT trainers

Training people on information systems and software packages has its own set of challenges. Perhaps even more so than with other types of training, preparation is the key. Each learner should have a terminal of their own on which to practise what they have learnt. This puts a heavy load on the trainer as he has many learners, often at different levels of expertise, with parallel needs for assistance. Nobody should be idle, so this involves building three levels of exercise to follow up each learning point – one that everybody on the course should be able to do, one that stretches most of the learners while the trainer helps the least advanced, and a third that will occupy the most advanced of learners and keep them out of mischief!

Trainer certification/professional certification

In some organizations it is perceived to be appropriate to be a 'certificated' trainer with a certificate from an organization such as the CIPD (see Appendix 2), or from a private organization that represents the best efforts of trainers in a particular niche. This certificate indicates a level of competence that is transferable across organizations. This is particularly common in the world of IT training, where many trainers and training organizations are accredited by the Institute of IT Training.

Trainer licensing

Some consultancies develop training and then make it available to organizations that need to adequately train the trainers who will deliver to the remaining staff. There is often a system of 'trainer licensing' bestowing accreditation on a trainer when she is competent as a trainer on the particular product. Such licensing situations may offer tremendous value to the trainer as she is supplied with first-rate materials and a train-the-trainer manual specifically geared to the product.

Additional 'licensing' need may be forthcoming in other circumstances, such as with a legal requirement such as food hygiene, or financial services or a global programme requiring multi-language delivery.

Using external speakers

If you are using an external speaker there are a number of factors to consider:

- Why are you using a speaker? What are your objectives? What do you hope the speaker will add to the event?
- Identify the area of expertise required and set the objectives.
- Identify potential speakers; at this stage look internally as well as at external providers.
- Having identified potential speakers, narrow your choice by identifying their fee, their specific area of expertise and availability.
- Once satisfied with these details, confirm with the speaker the date, the timings, the venue and outline content. Clarify their details for any publicity material that you plan to produce.
- Be aware that, once booked, the speaker may require a cancellation fee if you subsequently call off the event.
- Matching a speaker to an audience is very important. Speakers vary enormously in style, approach and content detail. Their fee will also vary depending on their status.
- It is important to find a speaker who has been recommended, depending on the size and scale of the event. An uninspiring speaker can be very demotivational and damage your reputation.
- Prior to the event send the speaker the same details as the learners.
- In addition, out of courtesy, you may wish to send the speaker copies of your aim and objectives, the programme outline and your introductory content. If there is more than one speaker, you may wish to send each of them outline details of each other's presentation, or ask them to contact each other to ensure that they do not overlap each other's content.
- Prior to the event ask them for their equipment requirements and, like the learners, any special dietary needs. Also ask for hard copies of their slides, ideally before the event, so that you can include them in the learners' guide.
- Confirm that they have the details of the venue and establish their travel arrangements.
- Always write and thank them for their input after the event.

Organizing venues

Like speakers, organizing venues takes time and patience to get right, and often forms part of the trainer's role. If you have administrative back up, it is something that can be learnt once you have established the guidelines. You need very clear criteria to help you identify your ideal venue.

First, identify what you require in terms of the venue, which will vary depending on your event. If it is an in-company programme, you may have to use in-company facilities; however, increasingly organizations are prepared to use off-site facilities if they feel it is important to create different environments for the learning.

If you are going outside, shop around to find the best prices and range of facilities in your local area. Sometimes organizations want a venue that is further afield, and you are then reliant on brochure information or the recommendations of others. If you have an established network of other trainers or other company contacts, you can hopefully ask for advice from them.

There are some specialized venue-finding organizations that will identify your needs with you and then give you a range of options. Normally there is no charge for this service as they receive commission from the venue. They can be a valuable resource because they can negotiate on your behalf, and if you use them on a regular basis they will begin to understand your needs. Alternatively, you or your administration can build up your own file of contacts.

Although time-consuming, finding the right venue is very important for any event, but is particularly important when running a residential one, or a conference, because of the additional requirements in terms of numbers attending or the facilities required. You need to research the venue under the following headings.

Main room

- Is it large enough, and well ventilated with natural light?
- Is the seating comfortable, with a facility for the learners to write on?
- Are there syndicate rooms nearby?
- Are there toilets nearby?
- Is there a business centre, or somewhere where you can photocopy or send and receive faxes?
- Are there any likely planned disturbances, eg refurbishment, decorating or rebuilding?
- Are other large events being organized at the same time at the venue? (Sometimes small events can be overwhelmed by other, large conferences.)

Refreshments

- How are the refreshments organized? Will coffee/tea be available in the room? Can they be available all day if required?

- Is there a separate facility for a buffet lunch? Can you have part of the dining room kept separate for your group? This is particularly important for a residential event, where people prefer to eat together away from other guests. Some venues have private dining room facilities.
- What additional refreshments are available: mineral water, squash, mints, biscuits, cakes, fruit, etc? How are these items costed? What's included in the rate, what is additional? It is very important to establish the real costs when comparing one venue with another. Benchmark a variety of venues.

Accommodation

The standard of accommodation is another important feature at a training event. This too needs to be checked and the following questions asked:

- What are the standard and quality of the rooms included in the day learner rate?
- Where are the rooms located? You ideally want accommodation that is free of airport and traffic noise.
- Most hotels have a standard of accommodation that is expected by corporate learners, ie double rooms with single occupancy, en-suite, television, tea-making facilities and sometimes a mini-bar. While not every organization may wish to provide this level of hospitality, people normally expect reasonable sleeping accommodation with a minimum level of facilities.
- Increasingly people expect there to be some form of leisure facility, particularly if it is residential. This can vary from a swimming pool or fitness suite to golf, or tennis. Whatever facilities you require it is important to confirm everything in writing and to identify a contact person with whom you can liaise both prior to and during the event.

Further information is available in Thorne (1998) *Training Places: Choosing and using venues for training* (see Recommended Reading).

Dealing with the unexpected

However well prepared you are, you may find yourself having to deal with the unexpected. We list below some of those situations.

Handling learners' resistance or reluctance

Despite your best preparation and working in your most facilitative style, you may find yourself in a situation when you have to handle learner resistance. There may be a number of reasons for this:

- lack of notice about a training event or resentment at being 'sent';
- nervousness on learners' part about attending;
- not wanting to be 'shown up' in front of peers;
- personal reasons unrelated to the event;
- personal chemistry issues between learners, or between learners and the trainer;
- issues with the organization or the management.

Any of the above can create tensions within the learning environment/ training room. This may manifest itself in many ways, sometimes by a learner not getting involved in the course, or by a learner arriving late, wanting to leave early, or creating verbal challenges. A learner may show a lack of interest or possibly challenge the trainer, demonstrating 'When you cannot reach me, you cannot teach me.'

The event itself, including the trainer, can be questioned through comments such as, 'You don't understand our situation', 'Your examples wouldn't work in our set-up' or, 'This has been tried before and the management didn't follow it through.' The flow of a training session can be disrupted when learners want to vent their own issues.

Our suggested strategies for coping with these situations are split over four areas.

1. Before the training event

Part of the pre-event planning should involve identification of any potential organizational issues. Talk to learners' managers, ensuring that the managers and the learners are clear about the importance of the course and that learners are being prepared appropriately. Discuss any potential issues with the managers, particularly if there are personal or organizational circumstances that may influence your event.

2. At the start of the event, in the training room

Establishing some ground rules at the start of the event can help in terms of mutual respect and support. Demonstrating that you understand organizational issues, being flexible and adaptable in the way that the course is structured, allowing regular breaks and organizing access to all-day refreshments will all help to create an environment that is conducive to learning and supportive to the learners. Simple strategies such as asking the learners what they hope to gain from the event should identify areas of common ground. This works best as an interactive session, writing up their suggestions on a flipchart and being very honest about what will be covered and what needs to be addressed outside of the event or potentially on a one-to one basis. Remember that this does imply a commitment to try to meet their needs. It is easy to fall into the trap of identifying their needs only to ignore their input and to carry on and deliver the content that you had in mind with no further reference to their ideas.

3. During the training event

Once the event has started, the intuitive trainer will be working to develop positive relationships with the group, recognizing when the group needs a break and all the issues about attention span. Hopefully in the design and planning of the event there will be variety in pace and content, but don't be afraid to change the plan if the learners are not responding positively. If you are co-tutoring, recognize the support that the other trainer can offer; by mixing and matching styles and approaches, the learners' interest can be maintained.

Once you understand the cause of resistance, you can plan to handle it. All trainers need to be aware of their own natural fears, including 'Am I good enough?', 'Have I the authority I need?' and 'They don't like me.' It is key not to take situations personally and to consider the reasons behind challenging situations. Experience helps with these situations, but first courses can be daunting – an excellent reason to run pilots and to build in feedback sessions within the event and, if possible, co-train with an experienced facilitator. Remember your sources of confidence, keep eye contact with your learners, move closer to them and discuss their issues. All our coping strategies rely on our ability to keep our cool and our ability to choose the appropriate response to the situation. Fear can result in our making the wrong choice.

We need to be aware of the form the resistance is taking, being alert to what is happening at all times during the course. We will *sense* resistance, *see* resistance when someone is not participating, sitting back, arriving late, not paying attention or distracting others, and *hear* resistance with muttered comments, direct challenges and hostile comments in small groups, as well as unnatural periods of silence. We need not be paranoid, judging that the first time something happens (or is said, asked or refused) we accept it at face value, the second time become diligent, and the third time believe it to be resistance and take action.

If there is a general feeling of discontent or restlessness, be prepared to take time out to identify the cause. You may need to refer back to the objective and main agenda of the event including the learners' expressed needs and, adult to adult, seek to identify the reasons for lack of concentration and establish a joint commitment to work together to overcome any issues.

With an individual attempting to disrupt the event, you need to exercise mature judgement on the best course of action. Ideally you need to take time with the particular person, one-to-one, to identify what the real issues are. Sometimes people are unaware that they are being overbearing or taking up too much airtime in a group discussion. If there is an opportunity to play to people's strengths, ask the more experienced members of the group to allow others to contribute; this can be another way of avoiding direct confrontation. The last thing that you want to occur is an open 'spectator sport' between a trainer and a learner. If the situation becomes particularly difficult, suggest a coffee break and handle the situation one-to-one with the particular learner. During the coffee break take the individual aside and try to identify the root of the issue. If it is appropriate, allow the individual to suggest he or she leaves the course – hopefully this will only occur as a last resort. (Additional coping strategies can be found in Chapter 2 in the section, Handling difficult people.)

4. Following the event

As highlighted elsewhere in this book, it is really important that you carefully review all training events; as well as the formal evaluations, you should undertake your personal review or review the event with your co-trainer. You should always be running a 'sense check' during any event, recognizing the signals and trying to be in tune with the needs of the learners. Regularly discuss progress with the programme sponsors and be open to any feedback that they have received. Equally, even with careful preparation and with all possible care on your part, there may be events that are less successful than others. The important factor is to learn from the experience, seek to identify areas for improvement, and work to make sure that at the next event the lessons learnt can be applied in the new context.

Coping with nerves

Running a training programme is very much like a stage performance. Trainers often experience nervousness before an event, and the same exhilaration or adrenaline 'high' during a programme is often accompanied by a 'low' as you come down to earth. With experience you learn to adjust, but these mood swings can be disruptive for new trainers.

Fear normally occurs when people feel unprepared, and the better prepared you are, the more confident you will feel. If training is new to you, or you are preparing for a particularly prestigious event, the following may be helpful:

- It is important to prepare physically for the event. However nervous you feel, try to sleep normally before the event, particularly earlier in the week. Try to avoid too many stimulants – caffeine, etc.

- Make sure you know what you are going to say, and don't over-complicate what you are presenting. If you are worried that you might stumble over words, take out anything that causes you a problem in your dry run.

- If you do stumble, don't apologize. Pause, take a deep breath and continue. Everyone makes mistakes from time to time, and it will always seem worse to you than to your audience.

- Check the equipment beforehand, but also have back-up notes so you can cope if there is a problem with it.

- Do your research. Spend time understanding the company's objectives and the needs of the group. Try to meet some of the learners before the event as part of your design stage. Make references to their business. People appreciate it when you appear to understand their business and it gives your input a more tailored approach.

- Learn a good breathing exercise and practise it regularly. Relax just before you are due to make your presentation, particularly your shoulders. If you have the opportunity, go somewhere quiet and just think about your opening sentences. If not just look down at your notes a few minutes before you are due to start.

- At a large event, if you prefer not to look directly at your audience, instead focus on something at the back of the hall just above their heads. This will give them the impression that you are looking at them, but it will not distract you.

- Try to be as natural as possible. Keep a level of humour that seems appropriate; remember the other times when you have been successful – and *just do it!*

Problems with the venue

Regular checking to clarify details and confirming everything in writing helps to avoid problems; however, the key is not to make assumptions but always to check. Try to visit the venue, or obtain recommendations from others. Be wary of room size, because sometimes this has an impact on the proposed layout. Ideally, ask for rooms with natural light; check heating, air-conditioning and soundproofing, particularly if it is a room with thin partitions.

If, despite this, the room really is unsuitable, try to negotiate for another. This may be difficult if it is a busy venue, which is why it is much better to try and view the room beforehand. Over a period of time you will build up a list of preferred venues.

The same applies within companies. Work towards achieving dedicated space that is suited to training events. Whatever difficulties you experience, do not let this interfere with your presentation. Your learners will forgive accommodation and catering difficulties, but not an uninspiring event – then they really will have grounds to complain. Always be professional and put your complaint in writing, and try to negotiate a reduction in the fee.

Problems with the equipment

Most of the problems with equipment or the venue are prevented by good preparation. However, even with preparation things can occasionally go wrong. If any of the equipment fails you, hopefully you can carry on, particularly if you have a learner guide with the computer slides copied. If the video fails, you may have to talk through the broad areas of content, or move it to a later part of the programme while the machine is repaired.

Always ask for help quickly rather than entertain the learners with your attempts to make the machine work! You need to remain calm, and if the day is well structured the failure of one component can be overcome.

Non-arrival of materials

You should always check that the materials have arrived after dispatch. However, sometimes they go missing within the venue after arrival. Finding them is a bit like solving a murder mystery. You will have to painstakingly establish who delivered them and where, who received them and at what time, who signed for them and where they were put. If you have taken a hard copy with you, you can at least run the first session with photocopies while the search continues.

Emergencies

As a matter of course you should always check the emergency procedures at every venue and such things as fire exits, assembly points and first-aid facilities. An awareness of others' safety and survival should be your number one priority, and even if it seems like only a fire drill, you should ensure that all your learners leave the building and take with you a list of the learners' names. Wait to be told before re-entering the building. In today's environment of uncertainty it is particularly important to ensure that everyone is aware of all evacuation procedures.

Coping with illness

Occasionally illness occurs during the event; again you have to take a judgement on this.

There can be very different motivations and reasons behind this, but you should never take risks with people's health. This can vary from the need to call emergency services or arranging for someone to go to A&E, through to allowing people time in their room or suggesting that they may need to go home. Whatever the circumstances, always act responsibly, and inform their line manager and the hotel.

Security

Training programmes present a number of security problems. The learners have often come to a strange building where other members of the public are allowed. During the course of the day it is likely that they will be taking off their jackets, and handbags and briefcases may be left unattended as people move from room to room undertaking activities. You need to encourage people at the start of the day to be vigilant. Arrange for the door of the training room to be locked at lunchtime, and encourage learners to take their wallets and valuables with them.

Look after your own possessions and try to place them in a secure place, as you are more likely than anyone else to be moving around from one syndicate room to another. If anything is stolen inform the security officer within the building immediately and allow the learners affected to contact their banks and credit card companies, if necessary.

Cars stolen, damaged or broken down

Again, the person affected is not going to be concentrating on the event. Allow them time to contact the relevant emergency service, but encourage them to rejoin the programme while repairs or investigations take place.

Lack of learners

Sometimes, for a variety of last-minute reasons, the numbers that turn up are severely reduced. One or two fewer people, or equally one or two more than are expected, should present no problem. However, a dramatic drop in numbers may mean that the programme is no longer viable in terms of interaction or sharing of best practice. On these occasions you have to make a series of judgements:

- If the programme is part of an internal roll-out programme, are there others nearby who could be released to attend? Always clear this with their line managers.
- Has everyone arrived, are any just late?
- When is a group too small? It is possible to run an event with small numbers, but it is likely to be less effective, because people have less opportunity to share other people's experiences. Success also depends on your experience, as a more experienced trainer can turn a small group into a coaching session.

Sometimes you have to take a decision to postpone or cancel an event. Ideally this decision should be taken before the day of the event to avoid anyone making an unnecessary journey. Once you find out that numbers are low, try ringing around for any likely extra people. If it is an internal programme talk to the sponsor and the line managers.

In today's climate, running a training event is an investment and as such should be treated with respect and commitment. This takes time to achieve, and some internal functions battle to have training taken seriously. Therefore the more professional and businesslike you are, the more likely people are to take the training seriously.

As a trainer you always have to be prepared for the unexpected, although most events happen without any problems. Preparation and identifying venues that are able to respond to your needs are the keys. It is essential to keep a balanced and professional approach, but if you do experience difficulties, ask to see the duty manager, who often will be able to solve them for you.

6

Sources of Inspiration

Being creative

How creative are you?

One of the key skills of a trainer is the ability to design training programmes and learning experiences that are innovative, exciting and fun.
You also have to recognize individual learning styles and respond to the
needs of the business. Often you will also be faced with learners who
have arrived at an event with business pressures still on their minds. This
process is repeated over and over again in a trainer's working year.

For a trainer this means that you need tremendous energy and
personal strength to respond to the myriad of demands that you deal
with in your work with groups. You need to be able to think around problems and issues, to rise above what is ordinary to produce extraordinary
results. This is particularly relevant in organizations where the trainer is
being encouraged to become an internal consultant (see Chapter 10).
People will be looking to you for inspiration; they will expect you to be
outward looking and to be able to facilitate groups where new ideas are
generated.

Creative and innovative people have energy; they practically run to
places because they cannot wait to start things. They are animated,
excited and they may think of many more ideas than they actually have
the time to implement. They often work hard and play hard and in the
playing often come up with even more innovation! However, not
everyone has this energy; some of us have to work at it, so where do you
start?

Ideas generation

In Chapter 2 we discussed the importance of getting to know yourself and your preferred way of operating. The same applies to creativity and ideas generation: with experience you will begin to identify when you get your best ideas. Many people feel that often their best ideas occur when they are least expecting it, or doing something else. They rarely happen to order. Given the fact that most of us cannot afford the luxury of just waiting for ideas to happen, we often need to help the process a little.

From the minute you know you have to generate ideas, to be creative, or to design a programme, park the broad parameters in your mind. If you have the space, put the title or the development area on a large piece of flipchart paper and, using either Post-it® notes or felt pens, add the ideas as they occur.

Make things as visible as possible and keep adding. As the ideas begin to flow, even the most insignificant points may ultimately become an important feature of the end result. Also have with you some means of recording thoughts when you are doing other things, such as a small notepad, a Dictaphone or a laptop computer. Often your mind just races with ideas and you need to be able to capture them quickly before they disappear.

In these early stages it is important not to force the process, and if you find that the ideas are not flowing, leave it and do something else. Often people find that by doing something completely different their mind will suddenly start generating ideas. Creative thinking can also take place at night during sleep. If you focus on a problem before you go to sleep, something called the Theta process takes over and the mind produces its own solutions that are there when you wake.

Some people find it easy to generate ideas, but most find it a challenge. Everyone has a different approach, but we will share with you some methods that have been proven to work:

- Identify the times when you have your best ideas. Create the environment that works for you, perhaps a room with a special view and music playing in the background.

- Identify where you work best. Some people go away to write or have a special room, prefering to have their family or partner nearby so that they can break off from time to time to talk.

- Some people find that taking part in such leisure activities as swimming, running or climbing exhilarates them and helps the creative process.

- Equip yourself with the right resources, a bit like taking an exam: sharpened pencils, lots of paper, coloured pens, and so on.

- Spend time researching. Talk to clients and participants, visit resource centres and business schools.

- Review what has been done before, clients' material, your own material, videos, DVDs, books and magazine articles.

- Build up your own sources of material, everything from photographs and press cuttings to more structured items. If you have an idea write it up even if you are not going to use it on the immediate programme. It may be useful some time in the future.

- Set up a filing system, either computer or paper based; it should be well catalogued and cross-referenced and updated each time you develop a programme.

- Build up a network of contacts, other trainers, managers, consultants, mentors, people you know, who are a source of good ideas. Be generous with ideas and others will share theirs with you.

- Regularly undertake self-development: go to training events and learn from the trainer, be an active participant.

- Really try to think from the point of view of your client, trying to identify their priorities.

- Some people find it hard to be creative on their own and need to bounce ideas around with other people. Again, using a dedicated space with good facilities can be useful. Some design teams go to leisure centres, where they can combine a sports activity with thinking and design time.

The art of the possible

Really innovative organizations ensure that they are constantly improving. They encourage their employees continually to look for a better way of doing things. There is also a close link between senior managers and the workforce. In some organizations every senior manager spends time working at the sharp end of the business, while in others mixed groups of managers and employees regularly meet to discuss business improvement.

As a trainer or an internal consultant you may be called on to run sessions where people are asked to create ideas, often as 'away' days, where groups of people are encouraged to be innovative. As we discussed above, people often find it hard to be creative to order, and you can help by providing an environment that is conducive to ideas generation. Like any development event, the objectives need to be clear and people need to understand what outcome is expected.

The day, or event, needs to be structured to allow people to mix with others. You need to build in activities that help people to identify issues and to begin to find solutions. Even more important is to work with the organization before and after the event to ensure that ideas generated are seriously considered in the business environment. Too often people go away on an event and build tremendous enthusiasm and energy, only to lose it once they return to the workplace.

Many ideas founder because no one sponsors them. Sometimes organizations have product champions, which may be teams of people, but that should always include a senior manager or a member of the executive who can ensure that the business takes the idea seriously. Equally, product champions throughout the business can ensure that at every level there is a commitment to developing the idea further.

Running an ideas-generating event

As we discussed above, in running an ideas-generating event you need to set very clear objectives as to what can be achieved. It is important to highlight that not all ideas generated will be suitable for immediate implementation. In order to maintain momentum and the motivation for the group, a process for planning the implementation should be agreed at the end of the event.

In some cases this may mean reconvening the group or setting up planning or design groups. Ideally, at the end of the event there should be agreement to meet again to review progress (this meeting may be quite brief), or if the event has been very successful it may become a regular part of the business calendar.

There are a number of techniques that you can use to foster ideas generation. Every trainer will develop their own preferred way of operating, but the ones listed below have been used successfully by many individuals and organizations.

Brainstorming

This is one of the simplest yet most effective techniques for working with groups. It is either trainer facilitated or takes place in syndicate groups. Using a blank piece of paper and a single topic or heading, you note as many thoughts as possible, randomly, without any attempt to rank or order. Write them up as single words or small phrases. Usually groups will generate two or three pages of ideas and comments before exhausting the process.

The technique is designed to help with the flow of ideas and there are important rules; eg no editing, no qualifying, no restricting. The concept works because one person's thoughts often stimulate others and, by not interrupting each other, the ideas flow very quickly. Analysis can take place later. The activity often also creates energy and an element of fun within a group.

(*Note:* some people are uncomfortable about using the term 'brainstorming'; one creative activity could be identifying another name for this activity.)

SWOT (Strengths, Weaknesses, Opportunities, Threats)

This is a way of adding structure to a brainstorm. By dividing a piece of flipchart paper into four and adding the headings Strengths, Weaknesses, Opportunities and Threats, a group may analyse their business, the workings of the group, future business potential, in fact any aspect that seems appropriate.

Strengths and weaknesses are often perceived as current and internal issues, and opportunities and threats as future and external issues. Once the areas have been identified, different groups can work on the outcomes, eg, 'What can we do as a business to minimize the threats we have identified?'

Mind-mapping

One of the most well-known creative and enjoyable ways of generating ideas is mind-mapping invented by Tony Buzan. Since the 1970s Buzan has been exploring the workings of the brain and helping people to understand how their minds work. He particularly has researched the works of Roger Sperry and Robert Ornstein and whole-brain activity (see Chapter 3). The uses of mind-maps are endless; some examples are as follows:

- note-taking at seminars, conferences, meetings, school/college lectures;
- summaries of visits, sales calls, monitoring/assessing records of observations;
- problem solving, decision making;
- planning and designing training;
- life planning, career choices;
- revision before exams;
- writing articles/books.

Although mind-maps may at first be perceived as a very creative and right-brained process, Buzan emphasizes the importance of seeing them as a whole-brain activity, and to ensure consistency in approach he has developed guidelines for the completion of mind-maps which ensure that you maximize the potential of the process:

- Words should be printed in capitals. This helps with reading back the contents.
- The printed words should be on the lines and each line should be connected to other lines. This ensures the basic structure.
- Words should be in units of one word per line. This leaves each word more free hooks and gives note-taking more freedom and flexibility.
- The mind should be left as free as possible, and therefore you shouldn't worry too much about sequencing or order. The key is to capture thoughts as quickly as possible, but where possible use hierarchy and numerical order in your layout.
- Buzan recommends drawing a coloured image at the centre to focus the eye and the brain.
- Use of illustrations and colour can also add to the imagery.

One of the great advantages of mind-maps is that large amounts of information can be summarized on one page, and from this initial map project plans can be developed. Certain aspects can be given to particular people for further development, but you always retain a very visual model of the total picture and also the start of the process.

Mind-maps are now widely recognized in business training and education circles, and further information about their uses is available from Tony Buzan (see Appendices 2 and 3). Although this is a very creative technique, be mindful that not everyone is an enthusiastic supporter. If you are working with others who find this difficult be mindful of the content of Chapter 3 and the way that different people prefer to work. One of the authors has an innovation profile which identifies how people prefer to innovate and an organization's readiness to innovate (contact kaye@theinspirationnetwork.co.uk).

Creative problem solving

As we discuss in Chapter 10, HR/OD/L&D/Training professionals in today's organizations are often called upon to act as internal consultants or facilitators. One area that often requires support is problem solving. Problem-solving techniques are a common management tool, but applying creativity to problem solving often involves using many of the techniques that we have discussed in this chapter to encourage people to think 'outside of the box'.

The skilled professional will not offer solutions, but instead will use facilitative techniques to work with the group or with an individual in a coaching situation to enable them to reach their own conclusions on the best course of action. The following checklist can help the process.

Checklist for creative problem solving

✔ Qualify and clarify the problem.

✔ Agree processes/problem-solving techniques.

✔ Share known information (SWOT).

✔ Allow blue-sky exploration.

✔ Apply linear/logical thought.

✔ Take account of learning style preferences.

✔ Develop blue-sky concepts into practical outcomes with action plans for success using brainstorming/mind-maps.

✔ Allow gestation periods on all solutions.

✔ Share information.

✔ Explore options.

✔ Don't allow 'yes, but-ing'.

✔ Use when, where, why, what and how.

✔ Remember the customer's viewpoint.

✔ Consult other interested parties.

✔ Agree and implement action points.

✔ Champion the solution.

Networking

Recognizing the demands that are being placed on a trainer, there are some practical things you can do to help maintain your performance level (see Chapter 2). An important source of inspiration is other people. Being a trainer can sometimes be a lonely existence, particularly if you run your own business. You often have great responsibility for developing other people, and you are constantly giving of yourself, particularly if you are working in a high-performing organization.

In this section we look at networking as a source of inspiration. Every trainer recognizes the importance of generating ideas, concepts and activities that help people learn. Generating ideas on your own is possible but networking with others can be an invaluable source of inspiration.

Many informal networks exist around the country, where small groups of trainers either meet through professional associations or through other contacts to share best practice. Some of these networks are linked to industry sectors, some to voluntary groups, others are simply informal social events.

When people meet to share ideas or update each other on specific aspects of training, a high energy level is reached as they share concepts, visions and development plans. Sometimes these networks lead to mentoring situations. At their most creative level, people use the meetings to generate ideas, brainstorm or to identify future business opportunities.

Ideally, you want within your network people who match your learning style, people who will challenge your concepts in a constructive manner, and people who are just good friends, talking to whom makes you feel better. These people are invaluable in helping you to return to the real world after a particularly intensive training session.

Every trainer also needs at least one trusted fellow-trainer who will respond positively to those urgent late night requests for an ice-breaker or a team building exercise! The hope is that you too will respond positively in a reciprocal manner when they request the same of you!

As you become more experienced you may find yourself needing a special mentor, someone who really inspires you and will encourage you to push out the boundaries of your learning. It may be someone who has trained you in the past, it may be someone famous whose writing or whose video/audio tapes are a source of inner strength. Whatever the nature of the relationship, they provide the ongoing creative inspiration to enable the trainer to develop others.

As we discussed earlier in this chapter and in Chapter 2, it is essential for trainers to recharge their batteries. This is particularly relevant if you are working in a highly facilitative or consultative manner. Both you and your delegates will benefit from exploring this area.

Finally, remember that you too can inspire people. Sometimes we get so absorbed in the day-to-day work of training that we forget how much experience we have actually gained, often in a comparatively short space of time. Be willing to spend time talking to new trainers and sharing your experiences, the funny as well as the more developmental.

Offer to help others by giving them feedback, sharing in their brainstorms or helping them resolve issues. In this way you are giving to as well as taking from a network.

Using resources

Despite advances in new technology, many of the materials that a trainer uses are paper-based, which often takes up a huge amount of space. There are often rooms occupied with previous course material, reference books and flipchart outputs, all of which were once useful, or could be in the future if only you could identify what exists!

The nature of training is such that few trainers are immediately able to file and store resources at the end of the programme. Often the trainer returns to his office or home and drops off one load of material before setting off with another load to another venue. Inevitably this leads to material stockpiling, which then means constant searching to find useful handouts or exercises.

However tedious it may seem, it can be invaluable to take time to organize this information into a manageable collection that can be easily accessed. It will take many forms – some of it may be stored on a disk, some in boxes, yet more in a library or in filing cabinets.

The format really depends on the space and facilities available. The key is organization and the discipline to set up client files, subject files and a retrieval system that is appropriate to the subject matter. You should also distinguish between materials needed for activities that go into an activities box, and specific OHP/computer-generated handout material.

If your role involves presenting at conferences on particular subject areas, or you have a sales role, you will also have presentations that may be used on several occasions. Back-up promotional material may also be required. All this necessitates careful storing to allow ease of access.

Eventually it is likely that you will need a dedicated space labelled in the same way as a resources centre might be, where training material can be stored and filed either under a client's name or under a subject area.

One useful approach to organizing your own resources is to visit a learning resource centre, a library or a business school. Here not only will you see examples of how to organize your own resources, but equally you will have the opportunity to browse through their resources, and if you join as a member of the library or as a professional associate, you will have found a valuable source of information. Library staff can be excellent in tracking down information on your behalf; many libraries now have access to very sophisticated international databases.

Source materials should be an important part of your background research. Your learners will expect you to be up to date with new ideas and the latest business developments, and to have read the most topical and recent publications. Subscribing to professional organizations will give you access to other sources of information.

Many consultants associate themselves with universities or business schools to keep up to date with the latest research. Do not restrict yourself to information from your own country; look internationally too. Many organizations are thinking globally, and HR/OD/L&D/Training professionals also need to adopt a global approach in their research and development. There are opportunities for international research and to present papers at international conferences.

Whichever route you choose, managing resources effectively can be a powerful tool in ensuring your effectiveness as a trainer, and an ongoing source of inspiration.

If you cannot generate ideas, do something else. Relax, revisit your sources of inspiration, look for support from your network, and remember: no one is creative all the time!

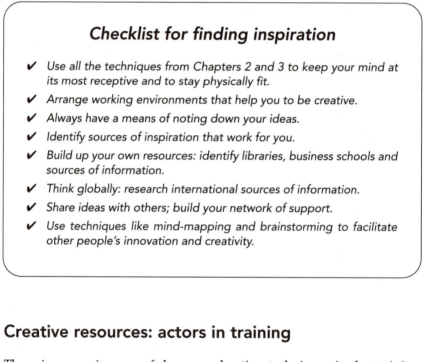

Checklist for finding inspiration

✔ Use all the techniques from Chapters 2 and 3 to keep your mind at its most receptive and to stay physically fit.

✔ Arrange working environments that help you to be creative.

✔ Always have a means of noting down your ideas.

✔ Identify sources of inspiration that work for you.

✔ Build up your own resources: identify libraries, business schools and sources of information.

✔ Think globally: research international sources of information.

✔ Share ideas with others; build your network of support.

✔ Use techniques like mind-mapping and brainstorming to facilitate other people's innovation and creativity.

Creative resources: actors in training

There is a growing use of drama and acting techniques in the training room, often using actors to supplement the trainers' skills. The major uses include:

- actors being used as role-players when training topics cause nervousness or inability of learners to reproduce the required behaviours;

- analogy playlets when a business problem is represented by a parallel situation played out by actors and then analysed with the help of a facilitator;
- forum theatre in which a business situation is depicted by actors, with learners able to stop and redirect the action; this allows learners to use the actors to explore their own difficulties in the particular situation.

For more information on this particular resource see the CIPD (Chartered Institute of Personnel and Development) website under 'Topics for Trainers – Theatre' (or Training comes of age), www.cipd.co.uk.

7

Developing Talent and Employee Engagement

Organizations often try to set up talent management processes, but real success comes when you engage with the hearts and minds of individuals. The organizations that achieve most success with this are those where the vision and values of the organization are aligned with the individual.

Fundamentally, talent development needs attention to make it happen. It also needs a holistic approach. Like customer service, quality standards and health and safety, you cannot just give the responsibility to one person and hope that it will happen. There has to be belief and commitment from the CEO and the executive right through line management to the newest recruit.

Organizations can convince themselves that talent management is being carried out when they create a system to define the steps, or outline a process to manage talent. However, talent *development* only happens when you create a culture based on shared values and beliefs, where thinking and feeling emotions are engaged and the leadership demonstrates its commitment through its behaviour and attitudes.

Individuals joining an organization need to feel that they are valued and that their contribution will make a difference. It is easy to say that this is happening, but far harder to have concrete evidence of its application.

In any discussion about talent development, or development of high potential, it is important first to *emphasize the development of all individuals*. No organization should focus all its attention on developing only part of its human capital. What is important is recognizing the needs of different individuals within its community.

In the search for an effective process for developing talent, most organizations recognize the need to do it differently; the challenge is often to identify how and where to start. Talented people do not necessarily fit into an easy system of classification. People are talented in many ways: some may have a particular aptitude for doing something, which may be primarily skill-based. Others may be gifted artistically, and yet others may demonstrate their talent in more outrageous ways and may be seen as maverick in their approach to life. We have worked across the whole spectrum of capability and have tried to draw conclusions that are applicable in the broadest context of talent development.

The bigger organizational picture

One of the most comprehensive and well-respected summaries of the key issues related to talent is contained in *The War for Talent* (2001) by McKinsey & Company consultants Ed Michaels, Helen Handfield Jones and Beth Axelrod.

Based on five years' in-depth research surveys of 13,000 executives at more than 120 companies and case studies of 27 companies, they identified five imperatives that companies need to act on if they are going to win the war for managerial talent and make talent a competitive advantage. These are summarized as:

'Creating a winning EVP (employee value proposition) that will make your company uniquely attractive to talent.

Moving beyond recruiting hype to build a long-term recruiting strategy.

Using job experiences, coaching and mentoring to cultivate the potential in managers.

Strengthening your talent pool by investing in A players, developing B players, and acting decisively on C players.

Central to this approach is a pervasive talent mindset – a deep conviction shared by leaders throughout the company that competitive advantage comes from having better talent at all levels.'

One of the major considerations in creating a talent development process is the ability to enable different parts of the business to talk to each other. As part of the background research it is important to capture a broad spectrum of views from the CEO and the board, senior and line managers, the current cadre of people who are considered to be talented and members of the HR team. Sample questions could be:

- How is talent defined and identified in this organization, ie what do we mean by talent?
- How effective is our recruitment process at identifying talent?
- What does our organization do to create a culture and climate to encourage the learning potential of *all* employees?
- What steps have we taken to create an environment where potential employees want to come and work for us?
- How should we attract, engage and retain talented people?
- How is high potential identified and sponsored? What do we do to actively champion talent?
- What do we do to actively encourage experimentation and allow failure in pursuit of a good idea, or new ways of operating?
- What steps have we taken to ensure that our management structure is developing new talent and creating a coaching and learning culture?
- Is our performance management system flexible enough to recognize individual potential and to reward unique behaviour? If yes, how is this achieved?
- Do we have a diverse and multi-talented workforce? How has this been achieved?
- How have we managed the expectations of talented people?
- What measures or processes have we put in place to assess the effectiveness of our talent strategy?
- What is our policy on redeployment; what do we do to encourage talented people to return to our organization?
- What is the biggest challenge in managing talent within our organization?

The above is only a sample of some of the questions that could be used in your background research.

Use all these data to create a proposal for your senior manager and, hopefully, for your executive board. It is important that any paper that is prepared follows the principles of any business proposal and clearly lays out the options, the business/individual benefits, the likely costs and the proposed timescales. There should also be an executive summary.

In examining the overall process of growing leaders, managers and expert talent for the future, you may need to establish the following:

- base-line competency-based criteria for the role of a manager and ways of identifying and developing management talent;
- additional stretching goal criteria that distinguish talent;
- ways of identifying and developing management talent;
- an accurate analysis of the talent that currently exists and the gap between where you are and where you would like to be;
- a development plan to increase the opportunities for talent to be grown;
- a review of the current learning and development opportunities offered to managers;
- other opportunities for talented individuals within the business;
- a method and template for succession planning across the business for expert and leadership roles;
- the key roles that need succession plans;
- a process for tracking talent and identifying successors/talented individuals for those roles.

Employee engagement

Another term that has developed in recent times is 'employee engagement'.

Research has shown that engaged employees are more likely to stay with an organization, be an advocate of the company and its products and services, and contribute to the bottom-line business success. There is a significant link between employee engagement, customer loyalty and profitability. Gallup undertook research and found there were 12 key employee expectations which, when satisfied, form the foundations of strong feelings of engagement and are linked to relevant business outcomes, including retention, productivity, profitability, customer engagement and safety.

As highlighted below, employees expect more from an employer than just a pay cheque at the end of the month. The UK lags behind the United States to a certain extent in the facilities it provides for its employees, but given the hours that most people work, more could be done to create environments where people *want* to work. Flexible working, job-sharing, being more accommodating to mothers returning to work, and recognizing the different lifestyles and work life-balance requirements of all employees are just some of the actions employers can take to create a more employee-focused environment. As a nation we are becoming more aware of the impact of diet and exercise. Incorporating some of this philosophy into the facilities that are offered to employees, along with a cleaner, more airy environment means that employees not only want to work for you, but it is healthier for them too.

In Chapter 1 we discussed the importance of developing an employer brand. As part of that process it is also important to recognize how to engage with a diverse group of employees. The profile of the workforce is changing; the expectations, wants and needs are different. Organizations are increasingly focusing on what they need to do differently to retain not only talented employees, but all employees.

The cost of recruitment can have a significant impact on the bottom line, but more important, if an organization has a poor retention reputation it manifests itself in a variety of ways. For example, in some service sectors, a number of companies often operate in a similar geographical area. Within this area employees often 'job-hop', using the experience gained in one organization to move on to another. It may be because the money offered is slightly higher, it may be because they follow their friends, it may also be because one company gains a reputation for being a 'better' employer. Identifying what makes a 'better' employer is one of the more critical actions an HR/OD/L&D/Training department can undertake. Do you know where your company sits in the local league of employers? How do your past employees describe your company when they are on induction courses with your competitors? Employee satisfaction surveys have a mixed response within HR departments and from employees themselves, but well-structured questions with clear improvement actions taken as a result of feedback year on year can provide a useful measure of the level of employee engagement.

There are some commonsense ways of engaging employees that have been already mentioned, for example:

- think very carefully about the messages that you are sending out to potential new employees through your recruitment advertising;
- recognize the opportunities that exist to create a positive employer brand through all stages, from the moment you send the acceptance letter to them joining the company;
- some organizations use the term 'onboarding' to describe a process of support for the new employee which starts pre-employment, and continues through induction and into the first few months of employment;
- following this period, maintain an employee's loyalty through supportive management and ongoing constructive feedback;
- provide real opportunities for progression: new responsibilities, new teams, cross-functional working;

- clear and visible leadership, showing each and every employee that they are valued in the overall delivery to the customer;
- providing the right development, the right resources and the right support to enable them to perform effectively;
- clear communications, using all forms of media, to ensure the employee really feels knowledgeable about company performance;
- playing an active role in the community, being recognized for the organization's corporate and social responsibility;
- working and playing together, having fun, recognizing achievements, celebrating personal, family and company success.

More information is available from www.employerbrandinstitute.com.

Succession planning

Finally, it is important to recognize the need for organizations to think about succession planning. Very few organizations devote enough time to developing a carefully thought out process for this, which would recruit employees, develop their skills and abilities, and prepare them for advancement, all while retaining them to ensure a return on the organization's training investment.

Succession planning involves:

- understanding the organization's long-term goals and objectives;
- identifying the workforce's developmental needs;
- determining workforce trends and predictions;
- identifying the key roles;
- matching individuals to these roles;
- setting stretching targets and development plans to ensure that the individuals selected reach or exceed expectations.

In the past, succession planning typically targeted only key leadership positions. In today's organizations, it is important to include key positions in a variety of job categories. With good succession planning, employees are ready for new leadership roles as the need arises, and when someone leaves, a current employee is ready to step up to the plate. In addition, succession planning can help develop a diverse workforce, by enabling decision makers to look at the future make-up of the organization as a whole.

Checklist for successful talent development

✔ In any discussion about talent development or development of high potential, it is important first to emphasize the development of all individuals.

✔ Talented people do not necessarily fit into an easy system of classification. People are talented in many ways: some may have a particular aptitude for doing something, which may be primarily skill-based. Others may be gifted artistically, and yet others may demonstrate their talent in more outrageous ways and may be seen as maverick in their approach to life. 'Extraordinary individuals certainly make life more interesting', as Howard Gardner said.

✔ Organizations can convince themselves that talent management is being carried out when they create a system to define the steps, or outline a process to manage talent. However, talent development only happens when you create a culture based on shared values and beliefs, where thought and emotions are engaged and the leadership demonstrates its commitment through its behaviour and attitudes.

✔ When reviewing your approach to talent development you need to examine what already exists. Take what works in your organization and build on it. Take the lid off your organization and look inside: what do you see? What would make you unique and different? How can you build loyalty? Do you know what talent already exists?

✔ The more collaborative and forward thinking organizations recognize that a motivated workforce does not need to be 'managed' in the traditional sense. What talented employees do need is guidance, coaching and the sharing of wisdom.

✔ HR/OD/L&D/Training should be asking, 'How do we manage our pool of talent to suit our evolving business need?' This links to ownership of the 'talent agenda', as 'keepers of the people strategy' and aligned with the business, you should be creating an audit tool: How much of what we need have we currently got? How much of what we need can be created from what we have already? How much of what we have cannot be used by us effectively over the next one to three years? How much of what we need has to come from outside – where are they now and how do we attract them?

(The information in this chapter has been adapted from *The Essential Guide to Managing Talent* (2006) by Thorne and Pellant, Kogan Page; see Recommended Reading.)

8

Getting the Best from Blended and E-learning

This chapter is one that presents the biggest challenge in keeping up to date. The advances in technology-based learning are very rapid; equally some organizations have yet to embrace the potential. Education is investing in blended learning and young people joining organizations from schools and universities may already be very familiar with a blended learning approach. Like most developments it is important for HR/OD/L&D/Training professionals to use their own networks and journals to stay up to date and to be able to present logical arguments for investment.

One of the most important factors in creating blended learning solutions is to recognize where they fit in the broader context of organizational learning and development. Much of the underpinning concepts of learning and development discussed elsewhere in this book have important relevance in the development of blended learning.

The potential of blended learning is almost limitless and represents a naturally evolving process from traditional forms of learning to a personalized and focused development path. Importantly, blended learning should not be seen in isolation: it represents one of the most naturally evolving processes of developing your human capital. Therefore any strategy to introduce blended learning needs to be considered carefully and positioned within the broader context of not just attracting, retaining and motivating talent, but also addressing the more compelling arguments of return on investment (ROI) and cost savings. An important part of this consideration is based on answers to the following key questions:

- What could blended learning mean to our organization?
- How does it fit with our overall business strategy?
- How could it help us to attract, retain and motivate talent?
- What other tangible benefits could it bring us?
- How could it help us achieve our business and personal development objectives?

So what does blended learning mean?

Blended learning is an example of how online or e-learning has evolved from its first inception. Before discussing blended learning it is perhaps helpful to identify some of the different components, first e-learning.

E-learning can be found through a variety of different routes:

- online learning programmes incorporating activities and information that are very similar to other forms of distance learning;
- online learning portals, which take people through a variety of online and offline provisions;
- websites that focus on specific product and service offerings, highlighting features and benefits in the same way as a corporate brochure;
- specific sites that allow you to download articles or tools, either free or in the case of particular tools on a free trial basis prior to purchase.

Some definitions

When one considers the e-learning component it is worth clarifying some of the language. Below is a short selection of some of the terms that you may hear. However, new descriptors are being created all the time. The only way to develop your knowledge is to talk to service providers and colleagues and always ask for clarification if you hear a term that you do not understand.

WBT (web-based training)

This primarily describes training packages that are available using the internet. Linked to this is the concept of virtual classrooms where again the internet is used to link up different individuals in various locations with each other and/or their tutor and training material.

In the virtual classroom, learners assemble at their own computers for a session. The material is presented to them via multimedia. In some programmes there are whiteboard facilities, which allow learners to contribute comments or even draw, type text or paste images and to see the end result. There are also chat-rooms, which allow people to talk to each other. This can be augmented by video or audio conferencing. It is also possible to share applications, when learners can view or work on documents jointly or alternatively can voice an opinion or answer questions in a test.

Synchronous communication

Synchronous communication or learning is facilitated by bandwidth, which provides a medium similar to the way fibre optics support telephone communication. Everyone needs to be connected via an intranet or the internet. Most communications online are asynchronous, using time-delay methods, eg e-mail or bulletin boards.

Learning portals

These are hosted by service providers that allow clients to access online materials held on a ghost server. Individuals may leave a corporate intranet and go into the internet environment to use one particular provider's materials, or a number of providers may be available through a portal catalogue. Individuals may also create online learning communities. Learning portals can also be built and branded to link from a company's intranet, so a user has seamless access from one to the other.

Learning object

One of the features of e-learning is the need to provide learning that is 'chunkable', often described as 'bite-sized' or 'just-in-time'. Part of the rationale for this is that the learning often needs to be contained within a few screens as e-learners have neither the time nor the inclination to stay in front of their screen for long periods of time. 'Learning object' is a way of describing these bite-sized components. They are also important because they allow learners to get exactly what they need to learn, and not information that they may have already learnt in the past. This saves time in training and in productivity for the learner.

Learning Management System (LMS)

An LMS provides the technology infrastructure for companies to manage human capital development by tracking employee training information and managing, tracking and launching all events and resources associated with corporate learning. A web-based LMS provides online course and event management, content and resource management, comprehensive assessments, enhanced skills gap analysis, content authoring, e-mail notifications, and real-time integration with human resource, financial and ERP systems. An LMS manages all training delivery types, third-party and internal, including classroom-based, e-learning, virtual classroom and technology-based training, books, videos and DVDs. An LMS also provides access to authoring tools, 360-degree assessments, learning content management and/or virtual classroom functionality.

Application Service Provider (ASP)

This usually refers to a hosted service, which involves 'renting' the software, for example an LMS from an external company, rather than installing it and managing it on an internal system. In addition to providing technology on a subscription basis, an ASP also provides all the IT infrastructure and support services necessary to deliver it to customers. ASPs typically host applications at a remote data centre and deliver them to customers via the internet or a private network.

SCORM (Shareable Content Object Reference Model)

The US Department of Defense (DoD) established the Advanced Distributed Learning (ADL) initiative to develop a DoD-wide strategy for using learning and information technologies to modernize education and training. In order to leverage existing practices, promote the use of technology-based learning and provide a sound economic basis for investment, the ADL initiative has defined high-level requirements for learning content such as content reusability, accessibility, durability and interoperability.

The SCORM defines a web-based learning content aggregation model and run-time environment for learning objects. At its simplest, it is a reference model that references a set of interrelated technical specifications and guidelines designed to meet DoD's high-level requirements for web-based learning content. These requirements include, but are not limited to, reusability, accessibility, durability and interoperability.

The work of the ADL initiative to develop the SCORM is also a process to knit together disparate groups and interests. This reference model aims to bridge emerging technologies and commercial and public implementations.

Personal Digital Assistant (PDA)

This refers to a hand-held computer that, using WAP (Wireless Application Protocol) technology, has the potential to provide mobile access to e-learning content. This is becoming much more commonplace in industry. In addition, PSPs (PlayStation Portables) are available.

Definition of blended learning

Blended learning is the most logical and natural evolution of our learning agenda. It can be supported and enhanced by using the wisdom and one-to-one contact of personal coaches. It is a mix of:

- multimedia technology;
- CD-ROM;
- virtual classrooms;
- voice-mail, e-mail, conference calls;
- online text animation, video streaming;
- 'blogging', where 'articles' are published online with the facility for readers to comment and also for company 'experts' to present a point of view;
- podcasting – either sound only, or sound and video (where the technology permits); sound can be used as an 'update medium' for people who have attended a course and need a short update when something has changed.

These are combined with traditional forms of classroom training and one-to-one coaching.

Why is blended learning important?

The real importance and significance of blended learning lies in its potential. If we forget the title and focus on the process, blending learning represents a real opportunity to create learning experiences that can provide the right learning at the right time and in the right place for each and every individual, not just at work, but in schools, universities and even at home. It can be truly universal, crossing global boundaries and bringing groups of learners together through different cultures and time zones. In this context blended learning could become one of the most significant developments of the 21st century.

So who needs to be involved and when?

This very much depends on the business and its internal structure. As a first step, it is really important to understand and think through the implications of embarking on a process of blended learning before figuring out the who and when. What are the immediate needs? What are the must-haves? Who will benefit in the organization and how will the organization as a whole benefit?

The following represent some key steps:

1. Strategic-level discussion paper. One of the major considerations in creating blended learning solutions is the ability to enable different parts of the business to talk to each other, for example the IT department and the training/learning and development department. In its initial stages of development it will be really helpful for these departments to be in communication so that they are able to work together to create a discussion paper to outline the potential to the executive. Initial discussions with suppliers can also help in positioning the internal business benefits or benchmarking in the context of either your business sector or the wider global community. It is also important to look at the costing of the proposal within the context of the other business priorities. Working with suppliers about the proposed phasing of the costs can also be helpful. One vital component that is often missing is the presentation of the ROI potential or cost savings within the business case.

2. Sponsorship from the IT Director and L&D Director or equivalent commitment and buy-in from the executive. As highlighted above, if the potential has been carefully outlined with all the business advantages it will be easier for the executive to commit to the development of blended solutions. Do not underestimate the need to build the case for the executive, who will be making the decision on new software and/or hardware purchases. E-learning is neither cheap nor easy, so the business case needs to be made on the ROI as a result of initiating a blended programme, or the cost savings from switching from one form of training medium to another.

3. Internal champion/coordinator appointed. As well as the higher-level support, blended learning needs an internal champion or coordinator who will be responsible for the day-to-day integration of online learning and traditional learning. This person, or team, needs to be not just familiar with the learning processes but also able to paint a persuasive picture of the possibilities and to be able to coordinate the different ways of learning into tailored learning solutions.

4. Discussion paper formulated into an action plan with clear account-abilities. As with any learning development initiative, it helps to be able to articulate the key stages and to outline them in an action plan and, importantly, to allocate key accountabilities. In this context the action plan will range across a number of areas, from internal marketing to individual personal development. If this action plan is linked to the potential outcomes it will be even more helpful in managing the planned expenditure.

5. Internal cross-functional team selected to work on creating blended solutions. One of the very real issues in the early days of the development of online learning was a lack of understanding of the potential of the technology available. To achieve meaningful blended solutions it is really important to consider fully the range of media available and to create the best possible solutions. It will also be important to help the team develop the broadest understanding of the range of learning opportunities that could be created using blended solutions. People in this group need open minds and must not take fixed positions based on their own preferences.

6. Undertake an audit of the current learning provision, analyse who is doing what to whom and create a relationship database. One of the real issues within large organizations is gaining a full picture of what is happening in learning and development throughout the business. This is further complicated if, as with many large organizations, some of the responsibility for purchasing learning and development has been passed down into the business. The larger the organization, the wider the span of control. Introducing blended learning can provide an opportunity to undertake an audit of all the learning solutions that are available within the organization.

7. Undertake research to identify key providers of online learning. Online learning is now quite an established technology, with many companies involved. Like any form of learning and development, it will be important to undertake research to identify providers that can meet your criteria. It is essential that you talk to companies that have direct relevant experience in implementing blended solutions – not all e-learning providers do. Also, it is vital that the provider chosen can demonstrate the ability to work in partnership with a number of other providers and is happy to share methodology.

8. Try to refine this list to invite three to five external providers to tender to provide a blended solution. It is not necessarily essential that you go outside of your organization to build blended solutions; however, for many organizations it is the case because there is not the necessary expertise internally to handle the total implementation. Part of the selection process will involve identifying what support is really

needed. This will vary enormously from one organization to another and may consist of you identifying the exact level of support required. This may include commissioning an LMS or buying an off-the-shelf online learning solution, or commissioning your own tailored content.

Once you have selected your provider there then follows the next phase of development, which is to start generating blended learning solutions. The process for this is detailed below.

What makes for successful blended learning?

In reality the underpinning principles of blended learning are no different from any other form of learning. The key criteria are based on the following.

First, identify the core learning need. Identifying the learning opportunity in blended learning is the same as identifying any learning opportunity. However, what is important is recognizing the need to provide the right solution for your learners. One of the real advantages of blended learning is the opportunity to be more focused and specific about the learning need. Increasingly organizations are recognizing the importance of tailoring learning to the individual rather than applying a 'one-size-fits-all' approach. We all have preferred ways of learning and, despite all the research and recommendations to take account of how people learn, many organizations from school to work still continue to provide blanket solutions. As training solutions evolve into learning solutions the hope is that organizations will begin to recognize the importance of making the learning more appropriate for each individual. Blended learning provides a great opportunity to tailor the learning to the learner.

At this stage it is also important to identify how you are going to create the different parts of the solutions. There will be a number of ways in which the learning objectives can be met, and it will be essential that whoever is responsible for commissioning the solution has the necessary ability to look creatively at all the options. This particularly links to how the learning might be tailored. For example, if you have a very generic need it may be possible that an off-the-shelf product could be purchased. This generic provision, however, could be supported by personal coaching by a line manager, who could prepare the learner before the learning experience and follow it up afterwards. In this way the overall learning experience will feel more personalized.

Second, establish the level of demand/timescales. In any decision about developing learning solutions there will always be a need to assess the reality of the demand. However, blended learning represents a real opportunity to respond more effectively to individual demand and as such has an application that is as relevant to an individual within a very small business as it is to a team of learners in a large global company. The very nature of the blend builds in flexibility. As with the development of any learning solution it will be important to gain a real understanding of the shape and scale of the demand, not just currently but also in the future. This highlights the importance of making sure that those who are identifying the learning needs really understand blended learning so that they are able to ask the deeper-level questions to appreciate not just the immediate learning needs but the future needs too. It will also help if they can explore with the sponsor the potential of creatively offering different approaches to learning, including the full range of blended options.

Third, recognize the different types of learning styles. We know through the work of David Kolb and Honey and Mumford that we all have preferred learning styles (see Chapter 2). As well as considering the different learning styles, there are other factors to take into consideration in the way that people prefer to learn. A blended learning solution needs to take account of these factors. In fact a positive by-product of using blended learning is that it provides a range of learning solutions. It also represents a great opportunity to review and revitalize the full learning and development offer. Use blended learning as a real opportunity to ask yourself or your team the question, 'How could we really do things differently?'

Fourth, look creatively at the potential of using different forms of learning, eg matching the learning need to different delivery methods, and identify the best fit. One of the biggest criticisms of many of the early examples of e-learning was that they were either just technology applied to text, or technology overpowering the text. In the former the criticism was that people had simply taken words and put them on the screen with little thought about the real creative opportunities offered by the technology. In the latter the criticism was about the web designers who got carried away with the wizardry behind text manipulation and particularly animation only to find that learners were unimpressed, or frustrated by the time it took to download learning objects.

Like most learning initiatives, integrating blended learning represents an opportunity to take what exists and evolve it into a different dimension using new technologies. One of the first steps is identifying what exists. Depending on your size of organization this can be a comparatively simple or a more complex exercise. In large or global organizations it can be difficult to keep up to date with local developments. Learning and development professionals are a creative breed and a programme that may have been developed centrally can often evolve into something quite different as it is rolled out into local regions and districts, or even into different functions.

Tailoring to meet the needs of customers can also mean that the approach or content may be different from the original. Equally the wisdom gained through implementation may mean that what is offered is different from the original interpretation. All of this normally represents the healthy stages of implementation and development. However, if you are trying to develop a strategy to incorporate e-learning it is important to recognize what exists so that it can be integrated and formulated into new solutions.

This is where blended learning can really come into its own, by presenting the learner with a wide range of options. An important part of this process will be based on all the key stages above; in particular, the level of demand will be an important factor in designing the solution.

Fifth, work with the current providers, internal and external, to identify the learning objectives and to ensure that the provision meets the current need. In many large organizations this represents the toughest challenge, particularly if the different provisions are located in different parts of the organization either geographically or psychologically. IT implementation and creating an e-environment may not necessarily sit next to learning and development. If you are a strong advocate of classroom training, a facilitator or a one-to-one coach, you may not necessarily look for an online learning solution. The power of blended learning is that it can enable more elegant and bespoke solutions by combining one or more methods. The secret is to analyse what the key learning needs are and the most appropriate way of meeting them. In the early stages it may need some really basic examples of how it could work.

One of the challenges may be helping others adapt to the new forms of learning. If you feel that you excel in stand-up training, you may be less enthusiastic about adopting different ways of developing others. If you are fascinated by the use of design and technology in developing learning solutions, you may be less aware of the different ways that learners learn. However, in today's learning environment there have been a number of changes, including using the line manager as coach, shorter training sessions and the use of online learning and multimedia packages. Going forward, it will be important to help everyone involved with learning and development make their maximum contribution.

Sixth, undertake an education process and develop a user-friendly demonstration to illustrate the potential of blended learning. As well as the need to outline the potential of blended learning, it is also necessary to undertake an education process with the rest of the business; this will need to be far-reaching as it will include fellow learning and development professionals, line managers and the learners themselves. Some of the potential issues are likely to be linked to the need to do things differently and people usually need support with handling change, so it will be important to help people recognize the potential as well as helping them to identify the solution that works for them. There are a number of ways that this can be achieved, which can involve online demonstrations, PowerPoint presentations, small lunchtime meetings or workshops.

Seventh, be prepared to offer follow-up coaching support. Before e-learning became so topical some organizations had created learning resource centres. These centres provided learners with the opportunity to use technology to support their learning and development; in some cases large sums of money were invested in purchasing or developing multimedia solutions. One of the issues that determined the success or otherwise of these centres was the level of support available. This issue has remained throughout the development of e-learning and blended learning.

This support does not have to be through the same person. It could be a line manager who starts the process and continues to monitor progress throughout the individual's development. Individuals may also have a mentor; they can be encouraged to talk through their life goals with a partner or someone close to them. There may be an online support coach, peer support teams or different tutors linked to both the online and classroom development. The most important factor is that when learners feel the need for support they have access to the most appropriate person available for them.

Eighth, set up a monitoring process to evaluate the effectiveness of the delivery. One of the criticisms levelled at many learning and development initiatives is that they are not effectively monitored and evaluated. This can have significant impact when the organization is trying to measure the ROI. With something as far-reaching as introducing blended learning it is important to track the development, the lessons learnt and what improvements can be made. Having an internal Learning Management System can really help in this process.

Having identified the process, one of the major considerations will be the creation of the content.

Designing and writing online learning

The principles behind designing online learning are no different from those for any other learning intervention, except for the fact that online learning will constrained by what is technically feasible, the available budget and compliance to SCORM. As highlighted earlier in this book, everyone has particular preferences when learning. In designing the learning experience it is important to take account of these preferences and build a learning experience that provides enough variety to cater for this. The very nature of how we learn means that online learning can only ever be one part of a broader learning experience. Thinking creatively about the design, however, can mean that it can be stimulating, interesting and intimate for the learner.

Who should be designing the materials?

One really important consideration must be how to develop the materials. Although it may be challenging and interesting to develop web design skills in order to develop your own online materials, it may not be practical or possible within your time frame of introducing blended learning. There are a number of roles that you can valuably perform in the process, but unlike some of these, writing for the web is more specialized, and you must ask yourself if this is the best use of your time.

Guardians of intellectual property

One way of achieving a best fit is to recognize the roles and expertise involved in the total process. Internally it may be more appropriate for you to become a guardian of intellectual property, recognizing your breadth and depth of knowledge about content, the users/learners and the learning and development process. Externally there may be web designers and authors. By taking the expertise from the right people with the right knowledge it will be far easier to create a blended solution that has a higher chance of success.

Recording and protecting what you know

To protect your intellectual property it is absolutely vital to keep meticulous records of all the stages in development. One of the major issues is disclosure. You can issue confidentiality agreements and sign non-disclosure documents, but it is important to assess the level of risk you are taking when you start talking about your ideas and concepts. The best advice is to be careful, recognize the value of what you have created and take professional advice where appropriate.

Auditing content

Auditing and identifying where relevant content is located within an organization are also highly relevant. Benchmarking best practice externally and networking with fellow professionals is another important role. Assembling a team of sample users to pilot and test the material will be a major contribution to the final success of the product. Equally, introducing the concept of blended learning to colleagues and to the rest of the organization can help to ensure that the implementation is more successful.

Design principles

What the online component of blended learning shouldn't be is a training programme simply put onto the web. Used properly there are excellent opportunities to make learning interactive, dynamic and fun, but it does require the use of specialist design software and IT skills to create an effective learning environment.

There are some important criteria to remember when developing online learning. You can also use this as a checklist for evaluating material developed by others. It is important to recognize the following:

- Content should be high quality and interesting.
- Less equals more; remember your learner will potentially be reading off a screen.
- Think about print options; some information can be printed off to read rather than scrolling through a screen.
- Use a journalistic, conversational style rather than an academic approach.
- You can refer people on to other sites for articles and resources.
- Ideally use a designer to enhance your words on screen.
- Recognize that many people may be viewing your material on laptops or smaller screens.
- Make careful use of illustration and animation.
- Remember that, unlike with some other forms of learning where the sequence may be more controlled, online learners may be entering a screen in a more random sequence. They may also drill down into the content, so having clear forms of navigation will be important to help them find their way around.

As in the early days of video when people were coming to terms with the ability to photograph people moving, you now need to recognize the reason why you are using online learning. It should be giving the learner a richer experience than simply reading flat text. For much online courseware, audio is used to involve another 'sense'. The more senses involved, the quicker training objectives are achieved and the higher the retention rate. Where audio is used, text will typically merely provide summary/bullet points (ie the bulk of the information is presented aurally). If all you put up on the web is flat text, however well created, there is the question: is this the best way of presenting your information? There are distinct advantages in having the text easily accessible in an online environment, ie it is a lot more accessible than having to physically go to a library. Essentially the key message is use as many senses as possible and also make the 'blend' as rich as possible.

Contract with the learner

One of the benefits of an online environment is that it can create an intimacy with the learner, which needs to be respected. One of the issues with e-commerce has been a very natural reluctance on the part of the user to giving personal information when undertaking a transaction, and learning is no different. Once users have started a process of interaction they will be revealing information about themselves that should be protected and treated with integrity. The very nature of the learning they are undertaking may include them recording their personal responses to different situations; they may be undertaking assessments; they may be sharing their views with others.

Using other media

As well as online learning, there may also be other elements of learning that need designing, and the same principles apply. Whether it is a CD-ROM, video streaming, or distance or open learning, the focus must always be on the end user. Another question to ask yourself and the designers when commissioning any form of learning is whether it is the most effective way of transmitting the learning to the end user. Is it interesting? Does it take the right amount of time? Is the learning reinforced in different ways? Increasingly standards are being set, eg SCORM, so there is another layer of questions to ensure compliance with global standards.

Other key points to remember

One of the disadvantages of the growth of more technology-based learning is the lack of human contact; individual learners are losing the opportunity to talk through their embryonic ideas with other people. The whole philosophy of self-managed learning provides individuals with choices about how and where they learn, which has distinct advantages for both the individual and the organization. However, one of the potential losses from the reduction in training programmes is not so much what happens in the classroom or lecture theatre, but the learning that takes place on training events in those quieter, more intimate moments when two people start talking to each other at the end of a day, or in seminar groups before someone interrupts them and tells them to get on with the task. Therefore when introducing blended learning it is important to remember the need to include opportunities for this level of personal contact as part of the learning experience.

Working virtually

One of the distinct advantages of technology is the ability to transmit messages rapidly around the world. Globally, technological advances mean that organizations rarely sleep, working virtually. While Europe is asleep the business runs through the Pacific Rim, paying less for services provided by workers who are inducted into the culture of the country they are representing.

Below is a series of questions designed to prompt reflection and hopefully highlight some key areas of development that could make working virtually more effective:

- How often do we take time to think through projects properly?
- Do we use planning techniques?
- Do we have analytical thinking skills?
- We will need to plan this process. Have we undertaken a SWOT analysis yet?
- How creative are we? Are we hungry for information? Are we curious?
- Do we share ideas with others? Do we take advantage of global time zones to work virtually in teams?
- Do we use idea-generating techniques? Do we take time to identify what really inspires us?
- How open are our minds? How often do we say, 'Why don't we try this?' as opposed to, 'We've tried it before; it won't work.'
- What do our customers need that we don't currently give them?

- What do we have that works really well that could be adapted? What could we do more quickly or more efficiently?

- Do we build teams of people with different styles of thinking? Do we take time to explore how we can work together? Do we play to people's strengths?

- Do we tend to keep to the same pattern of working or do we regularly explore new options?

- When we are presented with a challenging situation, do we take time to explore the 'what if' and develop a plan for contingencies?

- Do we develop a worst case scenario and plan how we would deal with any issues that might arise?

- When testing possible links, do we ask 'Who? What? Why? When? Where? How?' Do we consider all the possible consequences of new product development and project management?

- Do we always consider the bigger picture?

- Do we consider the following: the strategic implication, the people implication and the customer?

- How often do we review the decisions that we have made?

- Do we allow time to review our assumptions before passing on our conclusions or decisions to others?

- Are we driven by a deadline or do we build in a contingency time that allows for reflection and consultation?

You may want to reflect on these questions or discuss the key issues with another team member or colleague.

One way working virtually can help is in the design of learning, particularly when designers do not need to be in the same location. As well as the application of this globally, it can also apply more locally. Disney uses a technique called 'displayed thinking', where projects that are being worked on are literally displayed on the wall. What this achieves is a number of things: people working in different areas can potentially add their own suggestions, but also it serves as a valuable communication tool. This same process can be used to share information with others using e-mail or company intranets. Again, as mentioned above, you can use techniques such as mind-mapping, Post-it® notes or other methods to transmit a lot of information simply. There are a number of advantages to this approach:

- It allows for the natural and creative development of ideas.

- A number of people can contribute at the same time.

- Using simple techniques, ideas can be commented upon, amended or added to, while retaining the original document.
- It is possible to work through different time zones and shorten the development time.
- Working in this way can help to forge global links and overcome cultural differences.
- Everyone can work at a time, place and pace to suit their preferred learning styles.
- To be successful, designers need to follow the same principles as mentioned above.
- The same disciplines of meeting deadlines and responsiveness also need to apply in this virtual environment.

E-technologies have particular relevance in supporting virtual teams. This can involve you in being part of a global team, or working with teams that are working virtually. Importantly, with virtual teams there is an even more pressing need to establish the ground rules for working together. This can include the following:

- identifying what technology support is available and how to make best use of it;
- agreeing the frequency of meetings;
- commitment to attendance, on time and uninterrupted;
- agreement of team rules, eg responding to e-mails, within a certain time frame;
- ways of using time efficiently, eg defining the purpose of virtual meetings;
- using other methods to share information, eg circulating material prior to a meeting allows everyone to come prepared to contribute;
- ideally from time to time physically getting together to form more substantial relationships;
- understanding each team member's expectations and needs when working virtually;
- constantly reassessing the opportunities for extending the technology support as systems improve, but using it appropriately, eg not using valuable conference airtime on something that should have been e-mailed.

By remembering these ground rules you have the opportunity to exploit the advantages and minimize the disadvantages of working virtually.

Useful contacts

There are many providers of e-learning information; one useful source is the MASIE Center, which hosts the TechLearn and the World e-Learning Congress. Its website is at www.masie.com.

Another organization is WOLCE. WOLCE runs an annual learning event that, as well as blended learning, encompasses all delivery methods of training, which is reflected not only by the exhibiting companies but also in the conference programme. WOLCE's website is at www.wolce.com.

You can also contact your regional professional associations, many of which will have useful contacts on e- and blended learning.

What are the benefits of blended learning?

Using online learning within a blended solution helps to focus on individuals and their interaction with learning technologies using the internet or an intranet. There are a number of advantages to be gained by using blended learning in its various forms:

- learning can be more targeted, focused, delivered bite-size, just-in-time;
- learners can interact with the tutor;
- learners can interact with their peers;
- learning materials are readily accessible;
- blended learning can make use of a variety of techniques by maximizing different technologies;
- blended learning can build on other off-job provision.

There are very few disadvantages, but there are aspects to be aware of when introducing blended learning:

- launch it on- and offline;
- identify the support networks, both technically with help lines and with coaching support;
- encourage learners to announce when they are engaged in online learning so that they are not interrupted;
- encourage learners to recognize how they learn best and to create a learning environment that works for them, which may be at work or at home;

- encourage learners to share successes and support each other;
- create learning that is stimulating and visually compelling, and recognizes different learning styles;
- integrate online learning with other forms of learning.

What is the future for blended learning?

The future for blended learning will very much depend on the pace of change in your organization and the level of commitment to doing things differently. Introducing the online components of blended learning does require investment, but the cost savings could be significant in the longer term. It also represents a very positive way of targeting learning and development. However, it also requires sponsorship and commitment at the highest level to exploit its full potential.

On the technology front there are new developments all the time. Some will work and others may be more experimental. One of the opportunities for online learning in the future is the development of hand-held devices, PDAs or PSPs. Using wireless technology the PDA has the potential to provide mobile access to e-learning content. The growth of the use of mobile phones that have other facilities means that in time learning could be available through an individual's phone. Learning could be adapted from the computer to a hand-held machine. If this is the case the learning would need to be tailored even further, but already text messages are becoming a very popular form of communication, and a similar technology could be developed to share learning content. Some universities are experimenting with the use of pod casts.

If organizations are committed to providing online learning there will be the need to explore different ways of accessing the material, particularly in areas such as manufacturing and service environments such as retail and catering.

Whatever the technological advances, one key message about blended learning is to remember to stay focused on the learner. It is important that the learner's needs are fully captured and documented at the start of the project and that any success measures are based around these.

(The information in this chapter has been adapted from *Blended Learning: How to integrate online and traditional learning* (2003) by Kaye Thorne, with additional input from two subject experts; see the Acknowledgements.)

Evaluation of Training

Background

Note: this chapter specifically uses the word 'evaluation' to discuss the mechanisms of reviewing, in the interests of improvement, all aspects of learning and development programmes. Often, the word 'assessment' is applied to short-term evaluation activities – such as when the learners on a training workshop complete a 'happiness sheet' to assess the performance of the trainer or when a coach assesses the progress of a learner with whom he is working. Strictly, evaluation is a word that is applied only to the longer-term measurement of a learning initiative's impact on business performance.

The importance of evaluation

This has always been a key topic for trainers and their management – particularly with regard to return on the investment in learning initiatives. Training/learning and development that is not delivering the expected results is likely to be potentially harmful to the organization, demotivating to learners and damaging to the reputation of trainers. Meaningful evaluation of learning and development allows you to monitor results and to make any appropriate changes. Meaningful evaluation also provides you with information that you are 'doing a good job', and allows you to celebrate your successes!

In today's business world evaluation has taken on even greater significance than in the past. We are constantly reminded that the business world is rapidly changing. Almost every organization in both the private and public sectors is making important internal changes to develop a more customer-focused approach. HR/OD/L&D/Training functions have rarely ever had such priority as in those organizations seeking to rapidly modify skills, knowledge, behaviours and styles of working of their staff. The rule for everything associated with learning and development in these organizations is 'business-focused, fast and flexible' and we hear expressions such as 'just-in-time' and 'just-on-time' training. Everything needs to be done quickly but needs to be done correctly, and using the correct processes of evaluation is of the highest priority. The key to success is in the choice of evaluation processes that can be implemented with minimum difficulty and then followed up with urgency.

Why then, with this need for emphasis on evaluation, do we see that not every organization gives it sufficient focus? Some will direct vast energy into planning, developing and delivering learning and development programmes, yet apparently direct minimum thought to evaluation. There have been examples of major training initiatives, costing large amounts of money and involving much precious resource, that have included almost no monitoring or evaluation. No mechanisms were included to monitor the potential benefits for the business or for the development of the staff. It will never be known how much of the money and resource was wisely used!

Evaluation is undertaken with the purpose of encouraging improvement. When evaluation is planned, it is done with the intention of analysing results and implementing suitable changes in a timely manner – followed by further evaluation. Such cyclical approaches – agreeing standards, evaluating, improving, checking standards, evaluating, and so on – are the bases of really useful evaluation processes for each aspect of the training and development process. The focus is on maximizing the use of resources, maximizing the likelihood of business success and maximizing the impact on staff motivation.

What to evaluate?

Organizations typically monitor their training and development operation to understand the extent to which:

● training and development objectives and strategies are aligned to the business;

● training and development initiatives are assisting in improvement of the 'bottom line' and in the organization's overall progress towards its business objectives;

- resources applied to training and development are being used in the most effective manner;
- specific components of the training processes, including the training and development function, individual trainers and individual training programmes are meeting agreed standards;
- specific training and development initiatives are appropriate for the staff for whom they are designed and are helping to produce the planned business results.

To ensure that the appropriate evaluation processes will be used, organizations need to consider the following questions:

- Which aspects of training and development should be evaluated?
- Against what standards should evaluations be undertaken?
- What mechanisms of monitoring and evaluation, both quantitative and qualitative, are available?
- What sort of changes to our learning and development programmes can be implemented as a result of the evaluation?
- With whom will trainers discuss the required changes?
- When there are changes to be made, who will make the changes and how will the results of change be analysed?
- How quickly can changes be implemented?

Once the appropriate evaluation techniques have been put in place, full records of the results of evaluation need to be maintained. 'One-shot' assessments of a particular training event are obviously important, but the real usefulness of evaluation will come from tracking progress against the agreed objectives of learning and development.

Checklist for evaluation

The following pages discuss methodologies for the evaluation of the key aspects of training and development. Trainers should use the following as an overall set of guidelines to consider evaluation:

✔ Do we have an evaluation plan for each part of the HR/OD/ L&D/Training process?

✔ Have we (re)confirmed what we are trying to achieve through our learning and development programmes?

✔ Do we have standards and expectations for the performance of the HR/OD/L&D/Training function that have been agreed within the organization?

✔ How will we record and demonstrate progress against the objectives of the function?

✔ Have we decided how we will maintain records of the results of evaluation?

✔ Can we quickly change the HR/OD/L&D/Training processes if we need to?

✔ Has the organization clearly understood our evaluation processes and the expected roles of delegates, line managers, etc?

✔ Have all the staff of the HR/OD/L&D/Training function fully understood the evaluation processes and their respective roles in the planned monitoring and evaluation?

Evaluation of HR/OD/L&D/Training functions

It is worthwhile remembering that it is not just HR/OD/L&D/Training that should be singled out for evaluation! The role, responsibility and business impact of every part of an organization should be reviewed regularly and rigorously. Each function needs to achieve its objectives within budgetary constraints in order for the overall organization to prosper.

Evaluation can, however, have a specific urgency for an HR/OD/L&D/Training function. In common with other 'service' functions, there is a danger of learning and development being trivialized and having its existence queried at times when there is 'bottom line' business difficulty. Unfortunately, this attitude has existed in too many traditional organizations, and the well-known adage about 'cutting training budgets first' can still be heard in some quarters. In resisting such dangers and in promoting itself as a vital part of an organization, the HR/OD/L&D/Training function must be prepared for constant and strict evaluation. Indeed, as a potential 'leader of change and improvement', the function should be encouraging evaluation to prove its own worth and contribution within an organization.

Among the ways that HR/OD/L&D/Training functions are evaluated are measurements of:

- the perception across the organization of the function's worth;
- the overall view from summaries of the feedback provided by learners following training and development events;
- the business effectiveness of learners before and after they attended a training and development event;
- the commitment and competence of the function's own staff;
- the usefulness of the function's operational systems and processes.

Consistently implementing these and other measurements and reacting to the results is a constant responsibility of the function. This can be particularly challenging in organizations where the business environment is changing rapidly. The willingness and ability of the HR/OD/L&D/Training function to be 'business-focused, fast and flexible' can be severely stretched in an organization dedicated to continual change and refocus. The function needs to be able rapidly to evaluate its current effectiveness and be ready to make quick changes in its operation in support of the organization. Below we discuss examples of evaluation processes that have been successful in assisting HR/OD/L&D/Training functions to initiate proactive evaluation and significantly to improve their service.

Evaluation methods

Evaluation for the HR/OD/L&D/Training function is based on the results from a number of measurement techniques.

The most frequently used of these techniques, which include a mixture of qualitative and quantitative processes, are outlined in the diagram on p. 133 and are discussed in the following paragraphs.

Establishing acceptable standards

If you are going to evaluate the impact of the HR/OD/L&D/Training function, then you should be prepared to define appropriate standards. Obviously, the function will be evaluated against the objectives and plans that have been agreed with senior management. There needs to be an emphasis on sustaining improvement month on month, year on year. The standards will be both the commercial standards applied to every function in the organization and specific standards concerned with the implementation of learning and development. Techniques to establish these specific standards are discussed in the final section of this chapter.

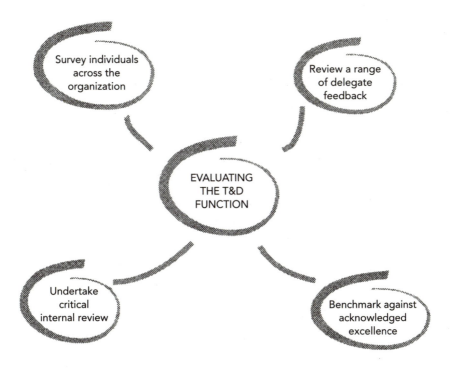

Surveying individuals across the organization

Ask a wide range of individuals from across the organization to complete a straightforward questionnaire (see Appendix 1). The chosen people should include:

- members of senior management;
- managers of functions that frequently use training;
- managers of functions that rarely seem to use training;
- a selection of recent learners and their line managers.

Look for trends as well as for the specific details that are indicated by the answers to the questionnaire. Identify particular situations that apparently need improvement. You should be starting to build a clear picture of those areas of the organization that would benefit from improved or extended services from HR/OD/L&D/Training.

A selection of the people who have responded to the questionnaire should now be interviewed. Choose those who gave 'average' answers and those who gave answers that varied significantly from the average.

As a rule, if people are interested enough to write additional comments on the questionnaire form, they are worth adding to your list of interviewers; they are showing that they have a real interest in your work. The results from this wide range of interviews will allow you to add specific knowledge to that built from the completed questionnaires.

Summarizing learner feedback

Learners in all forms of training initiative, including distance learning, formal training courses, performance coaching and mentoring will normally be requested to provide evaluation of the initiative. There may be issues that require rapid attention, but the overall aim here is to further understand how HR/OD/L&D/Training is generally perceived. All evaluations are collected and summarized and the results are carefully analysed.

The use and meaning of these learner evaluation forms is further discussed in the section on the evaluation of trainers.

Function reviews

This is an opportunity for HR/OD/L&D/Training management to take the team 'off site' and critically to evaluate the function and its usefulness to the organization. The prime sources of information for these reviews are:

- the agreed HR/OD/L&D/Training strategy for the function, which should include the current roles and responsibilities within it (see the section on the trainer as a consultant, Chapter 10);
- the results of all the evaluation processes described above;
- benchmarked information about sources of training excellence (see the section on establishing appropriate standards);
- the knowledge of the training world held by the team members.

Sufficient time should be made available to discuss fully all the information and its impact on all aspects of the function, and to make plans for progress. The meeting is likely to revolve around a number of brainstorming and problem-solving sessions using guiding questions, including:

- What are our functional objectives and how well are we discharging them?
- Do the aims and objectives of the function match those of the organization?

- Do we understand the business priorities of the organization? Is HR/OD/L&D/Training focusing on these priorities?
- Are we regularly checking that the organization's objectives have not changed?
- Are there business evaluation techniques in common use in the organization that could usefully be adopted by HR/OD/L&D/Training?
- Are we regularly updating senior management and our clients about our strategies, our plans and our current training programmes?
- How are we regarded by our clients and the rest of the organization?
- Are we making a real contribution to the organization? Could we proactively extend our contribution by offering new services such as coaching?
- What are the important gaps between what we are doing and what we should be doing?
- What, in priority order, should we be doing differently?
- Are we advertising our successes?
- Are we regularly researching and benchmarking externally to the organization to keep abreast of current HR/OD/L&D/Training trends?
- How can we present all the information we have gathered in a manner that will support our proposals?
- How are we going to gain agreement for these proposals from senior management and from the remainder of the organization who will be our clients?

At the end of the review the team should ask itself about the evaluation processes that are regularly being used by the function. Are they providing enough of the correct information to allow the function to evaluate and improve? Are there other, potentially more powerful evaluation processes that should be considered? Finally, the team will discuss the review process. What have they learnt in this review about the review process itself? Could it be improved?

The results of these ongoing functional review meetings should be opportunities to (re)confirm aims, objectives, strategies and plans with the whole organization, and the agreement within the team and with senior management on the manner in which the function will continue to be evaluated.

Modifying the training and development function

Modify those aspects of the function and its work that do need to change, and ensure that the organization understands what has been changed and why. Communicate with those who undertook the questionnaire, thanking them for their help and indicating the positive result of their input. Senior management should be regularly advised of progress, using summaries of your information in an interesting and digestible form. There should be an emphasis on the way that the function is continually being integrated into the business objectives of the organization. This progress report should be set against the current HR/OD/L&D/Training strategy and implementation plans.

Be prepared to identify where the problems really lie!

At the same time as you are surveying and reviewing all the HR/OD/L&D/Training processes, be checking elsewhere. If there consistently appear to be issues between the function's work and other parts of the organization, trainers should satisfy themselves that it really is HR/OD/L&D/Training that needs modifying. Fault and misunderstanding may lie within other areas of the organization. When an organization decides on new business directions or new internal processes, it can take several months for the new messages to be communicated. At any time there may be wide differences across the organization in the perceived meaning of the messages. Training should be reflecting the current needs of the organization, but occasionally trainers can be faced with learners who are not yet familiar with the new organizational messages. Be wary of deciding, and having others decide, before all the facts are known, that training and development initiatives are not supporting the business directions of the organization.

The way ahead

This section has so far discussed well-accepted methods of evaluation for the HR/OD/L&D/Training function. Surveys and benchmarking provide qualitative information, but the majority of the information made available by evaluation is quantitative. Trainers have always wanted to introduce 'softer' evidence to balance the weight of numeric information. We are beginning to see organizations where 'soft' measures of evaluation are being implemented. These typically involve:

- measuring the abilities of individual learners and teams before and after training programmes, normally against changes in competency;
- the use of staff satisfaction surveys and the measurement of staff retention levels;
- measuring operational performance against reference groups, for instance with groups of salesmen, by comparing the performance of a trained group with a non-trained group.

These soft measures are beginning to win acceptance, although there is strong debate about their real meaning! There are so many other influences in addition to training. Relating change to training alone is difficult to fully justify.

Questions and answers

Q *Is it really possible to evaluate a HR/OD/L&D/Training function effectively? Aren't there just too many external influences on the success of the function to make effective evaluation meaningful?*

A It certainly has always been a challenge to establish meaningful evaluation for all the aspects of training. Often organizations have not gone beyond qualitative evaluation at the broadest levels, and results have tended to be at too global a level really to assist. Basically, the HR/OD/L&D/Training function must be constantly evaluating its approach and its impact in order to implement changes to approach, in specific programmes, in specific training events. Unfortunately, the function too often needs to be seen to be self-evaluating for political reasons! It is currently still true that the methods will be mostly quantitative or qualitative at a very broad level; the skill of the trainer will be in the interpretation and use of the results.

Q *Where do we start?*

A As the HR/OD/L&D/Training function you are firmly in the world of client service. Most significant evaluations of a function will start by building an accurate picture of the organization's perception of the function. This starts by undertaking the questionnaire approach outlined above.

Q *What about continuous evaluation? Haven't we got enough to do in the HR/OD/L&D/Training function in reacting to the changing*

*needs of the organization in a 'business-focused, fast and flexible'
manner?*

A   All the techniques in this chapter should be used as an ongoing
process. The really interesting point for trainers is that as an 'agent
of change' there is a responsibility beyond the evaluation of the
function. There is a real opportunity, because the trainer works
across many areas of the organization, to be part of an evaluation
of progress towards overall business objectives.

Evaluation of HR/OD/L&D/Training programmes

When an organization introduces an operational business programme,
one of its components will normally be learning programmes with a goal
of developing the appropriate staff competencies. This is true for 'soft'
organizational programmes, such as management development, and for
'harder' initiatives, such as bringing a new product on line. The learning
programmes will be a mixture of initiatives, including training courses,
performance coaching and mentoring. Each of these will include evaluation procedures for the initiative to test success, including contribution to
the associated business programme. The design, development and implementation of these evaluation procedures will normally involve the
trainer working in a team that includes the sponsor(s) of the operational
programme and line managers of the most likely learners. The team will
agree the use of evaluation procedures that will monitor all the vital
aspects of the training and development programme:

● ensuring the training programme supports the organization's overall
objectives and is an integral part of the particular operational
programme;

● checking that the most appropriate methods of training and development are being used to achieve the agreed objectives;

● ensuring that the correct learners are selected and that the priority
order is agreed for their attendance on the appropriate training and
development initiatives;

● ensuring that each stage of the training and development programme
is individually evaluated to test that it is contributing fully to the
overall programme's success.

Checklists for programme evaluation

Below is a series of checklist approaches to implementing evaluation for training and development programmes. Our suggestion is that trainers use these examples to build checklists they can apply in their own situation. Disciplined use of these approaches, working with the sponsors of operational programmes and line management, will maximize:

- the possibilities of implementing successful evaluation procedures for all HR/OD/L&D/Training programmes;
- the possibilities of quickly detecting and solving problems;
- the chances of delivering training and development programmes that are acknowledged as making major contributions to operational programmes.

This approach will demonstrate the professionalism of the HR/OD/L&D/Training function and of individual trainers.

Checklist for setting the standards

✔ *Are there clear responsibilities for evaluation throughout the HR/OD/L&D/Training programmes and processes?*

✔ *What are the required contributions from HR/OD/L&D/Training to the individual operational plans and to the organization's overall business development?*

✔ *What other business initiatives and what other learning and development programmes are in place? Will they reinforce the learning we seek from our current learning and development programmes? Is there anything happening in the organization that could potentially detract from the impact of our programme?*

✔ *What are the learning objectives for the programme?*

✔ *Is it possible to identify critical success factors for each stage of the learning and development process?*

✔ *Who are the potential learners? What are their current abilities? What changes in their abilities are you expected to provide? Is there a priority order for the learners?*

✔ *What will be the most appropriate training and development method(s) for developing the necessary abilities?*

✔ What reinforcements of these new abilities are planned? Are coaching and mentoring programmes planned to follow the development?

✔ How will you evaluate the overall success of the learning and development and individual parts of it?

✔ What mechanisms will be in place to discuss problems and issues with the business sponsors?

✔ How quickly will you be expected to react and to make changes to the learning and development programme?

✔ What are the major risks to success? Have you discussed them with the operational programme sponsors? Have you agreed contingency plans?

Checklist for evaluating the components of the programme

✔ Are there clear responsibilities for evaluating at each stage of the learning and development programme?

✔ What standards are used in the design of training and development programmes? What mechanisms are in place to check if the standards are being reached?

✔ Are there clear directions to the potential learners? What will happen if the learners are unprepared for the learning and development event?

✔ What evaluation techniques will be used for each learning and development event? How quickly can you react if problems are detected?

✔ Is there to be a pilot learning and development event? If so, how will that be evaluated? When will it be? Will there be sufficient time to modify subsequent events if there are issues during the pilot?

✔ Have you agreed the formats for learner evaluations? What will happen to them at the end of each event? Are you clear how evaluations will be collected and used?

Checklist for evaluating the overall impact

✔ Who will take the responsibility for analysing the impact of the learning and development events on the abilities of the learners? Directly after the event and then after a further three months?

✔ Who will ensure the HR/OD/L&D/Training function receives timely feedback?

✔ How will the business impact of the HR/OD/L&D/Training programme on the organization and on the operational programme be measured?

✔ Who will summarize the result of the whole learning and development programme against the original plan?

✔ How will this be used to improve future HR/OD/L&D/Training programmes?

✔ How can it be used to improve the HR/OD/L&D/Training contribution to the organization?

Evaluation of individual training events

You need critically to evaluate each learning and development event in which you are involved. This is as true for a week-long course as it is for an individual coaching event. The more you evaluate, the more you learn, the more quickly the business will benefit and the more quickly your skills will develop. Each type of learning and development event will have its own type of evaluation, but each has the common aim of change and improvement.

Training courses

Each will have an overall aim and a series of specific objectives (see Chapter 4). These frame the expectations of the course's impact for both the learners and for the sponsor of the course, who is normally the business manager with whom it has been planned. As the course is evaluated, there will always be an all-encompassing question: 'Did it achieve its stated aim and objectives, and if not where and how did it fail?' In reality, the meaningful evaluation of a training course will involve all aspects of the course, from the impact on the business, through the learners' perception of the trainer's performance, to questions about the venue and the food!

End of course evaluation forms

These are a topic that will generate discussion with most trainers! They are traditionally labelled 'happiness sheets' and are regarded with lively cynicism in parts of the learning and development community. The cynical view says that the forms are no more than an evaluation of how much the learners have enjoyed their time away from work and how much they were entertained by the trainer. This view gives little credence to the significant improvement that can result from the correct use of the forms. However, the trainer needs to be wary of learners' reactions and may need to emphasize that evaluations will be taken seriously.

Although there are arguments that question their value, for most trainers and most learning and development functions the forms provide instant feedback on a course's outcome and on the perception of a trainer's performance. The trainer needs to stress to the learners that completion of the form is part of the course, that their input is meaningful in improving courses and is their contribution to business goals. If there are any examples where learner feedback has led to significant changes in training events or in training programmes, then discuss these with the learners.

Design your evaluation forms in a way that is appropriate to the event, to the learners and to the manner in which you will use the results of the evaluation. Often, most of the questions have numerical responses or are multiple choice. Ask the learners to spend time in thoughtfully answering all the questions, particularly those that need a full written answer. The example forms in Appendix 1 are designed to concentrate the learners' minds on the real impact and usefulness of the course they have attended.

If more than one trainer is delivering the same training course, use the 'happiness sheets' to monitor the difference between the ratings given to each of them. Why are the ratings different? Is it because:

● One trainer is delivering a course that learners are genuinely finding of greater value?

● One or more trainers are having difficulty in the delivery of this course?

● One or more trainers are having difficulty in building relationships with the typical learners on this course?

- Different trainers are using different training methods, or supporting the event in novel ways?
- Some trainers are managing to entertain learners and make friends with them in such a manner that poor evaluations are unlikely? This could be shown when the trainer is rated highly, but there is little indication of any commitment by the learners to do anything after the course or to change their working patterns.

The trainers delivering the course should regularly meet and discuss their delivery methods against the background of the evaluation sheets. They should be able to help one another to improve their individual performances and the course's contribution to the organization.

Using the results of evaluation forms

The summarized results of the training courses should be discussed with the sponsor of the training programme. Together you should decide on any modifications to the course and how they would affect:

- the likely level of benefit to the business from the learners using their new skills, knowledge and behaviours;
- the commitment of the learners after the course to put the learning into practice;
- any mechanisms that are in place to reinforce the learning of the course.

Other methods of evaluating training courses

The end-of-course 'happiness sheets' are by far the most usual way in which training courses are evaluated. There are other methods, some of which were mentioned in the previous section when we considered the evaluation of learning and development functions. These methods tend to focus on evaluation of the impact of the course on the learners. This involves measuring learner abilities before and after a training course, normally by using standards set by the competence bank adopted by the organization. These evaluations can involve multiple-choice checklists, written examinations or interviews conducted by line managers.

As experience of competencies is gained, these newer techniques of evaluating training courses are taking on more significance for trainers. You should continue to be aware of the concern that surrounds the 'soft', quantitative evaluations that were mentioned in the previous section. There are many different things that can impact a person's performance and attitudes, in addition to that of being a learner on a training course. It can be difficult, therefore, really to isolate the impact of that particular course. When appropriate, a follow-up with the learners after a period of time could be really helpful, both for the learner and to provide feedback for the trainer. The nature of the conversation could be built around their agreed action plan.

Pilot courses

It is normal to pilot a new training course, particularly when the course is likely to have a high business impact, and when a number of new training/learning initiatives are to be introduced. The audience for a pilot course should include learners with the same background and potential learning needs as the learners who will eventually attend the regular courses. In addition, pilot course learners may include other interested parties, typically members of the business function who have sponsored the course and other trainers who will subsequently deliver the course. Time should be made available for the pilot course to run one day longer than the planned regular course for which you are preparing. This will provide sufficient opportunity for detailed discussion of all aspects of the course and even, should it be necessary, for sections of the course to be tested more than once. Learners should be selected based on their ability to give useful and valuable feedback.

Evaluation during the pilot will be even more detailed than for the regular course:

- The trainer and the sponsor should agree SMART aims and objectives for each session, as well as for the whole event (see Chapter 4).
- Evaluation forms will be completed by the learners at the end of each learning session or each module of the course, as well as at the end of the whole event.
- The progress of the course should be reviewed regularly, either at the end of each day or first thing each morning.

Coaching and mentoring events

These sorts of events are generally one-to-one events as opposed to the one-with-many of a training course. Evaluating the progress of a mentoring or coaching programme, or of one specific session, should therefore be a straightforward process. The relationship that is being built is open and forthright, and giving feedback in either direction should be part of this relationship. As the format of each meeting is planned, 10 minutes is scheduled at the end to allow the coach and the learner to discuss progress and the coaching/mentoring techniques that are being used. These 10-minute evaluation sessions will employ the same skill sets that have been used throughout the coaching and mentoring session (see Chapter 10). The coach/mentor questions the learner's view of the success of the session and the learner's views of potential improvements in the coaching/mentoring process. The coach/mentor and the learner agree any changes and how they will be introduced.

An occasional session should be devoted to a review of the overall objectives of the coaching and/or mentoring. The trainer and the learner should agree that the objectives are still appropriate, that the sessions are working towards those objectives and that the techniques of coaching/mentoring in use are appropriate.

The trainer/coach/mentor should ensure that these evaluation discussions and their outcomes are recorded. This will obviously promote the success of the coaching/mentoring sessions and the perceived professionalism of the trainer. Also, the results of such evaluation sessions should be fed into overall evaluations of the trainer personally, the HR/OD/L&D/Training function and the techniques currently in use for coaching and mentoring.

Overall evaluation of a learning programme

This is at the heart of the discussion of evaluation in learning, particularly in relation to the return on the investment that is made in the learning programme. This is not simply the cost of the trainer's time, but also the cost of the facilities and materials involved as well as the consequential cost of having learners away from their workplace.

At the simplest level, return on investment (ROI) can be represented as a percentage, by subtracting the cost of training from the benefits of the training and dividing the answer by the costs of training. 'Hard' training lends itself to evaluation and ROI – we can train operatives and calculate the financial benefits in terms of reduced scrap or faulty parts. 'Soft' training is notoriously hard to evaluate in this way, the impact on soft skills being difficult to measure.

There are many who believe that the efforts in measuring ROI for soft training is actually a waste of time and effort should be directed into ensuring that the training is fully aligned to learner needs, well executed and is fully 'embedded' into the workplace after the training initiative. Evaluation is absolutely appropriate – working with learners and their managers to ensure that the training is fully planned and that it fully attains its objectives – but meaningful ROI is not possible. Embed training by techniques such as having the learner return from a course and discuss with his or her manager:

- What was *learnt* from the workshop?
- What learning was particularly *relevant* to this learner from what was learnt from the workshop?
- What does the learner now *intend* to do to use the new competence and what will he or she do to maintain and increase the competence?
- How can the manager *monitor* progress and assist in the implementation and development of the new competence?

Others firmly believe ROI calculations are possible and meaningful. The majority of models that link together all the aspects of evaluating learners – from their attendance on a learning initiative through to their 'bottom line' benefit to the organization – are based on the Kirkpatrick model. This model comprises four stages (providing a set of standards rather than a process):

1. Reactions: during and directly following the event, using facilitator questions and formal end-of-initiative evaluations by the learners.
2. Learning: as the final stage of the initiative, or back in the workplace a short time after the initiative, learners are tested by quizzes, job activity, in-depth interviews; this is designed to test understanding of the learning initiative.
3. Behaviour: the testing of the learner's enhanced performance in the workplace resulting from the learning initiative through specifically designed tests or, most often, direct observation by line managers and supervisors.
4. Results: the measurement of a contribution to the 'bottom line' from an individual or a group of individuals participating in a learning initiative. For a production staff member this evaluation is normally undertaken by monitoring times, error percentages and the like before and after the learning initiative. For a knowledge worker it could involve 360-degree feedback from customers, suppliers, line managers and team members.

Jack Phillips has built a 10-stage model for ROI that is supported by a number of commercially available suites of software (see Recommended Reading).

Evaluation of trainers

Those working for the majority of organizations will have annual performance management and appraisal systems available. Such systems provide trainers with overall performance evaluations and with agreed personal development plans. The organization for which you work may already have developed a competency model for your job and be using this for your ongoing evaluation and development. Here we are discussing ways in which trainers can evaluate themselves in the area of training competence beyond these general annual appraisals. The ideas are also applicable to other people, such as line managers who are asked to take on a training responsibility. The results of all of these evaluations should be added to the considerations of personal development and skill development plans.

The essence of the approach is for the trainer regularly to build evidence from a number of sources for use with a personal checklist (see Appendix 1), against which he can evaluate himself and monitor his own progress. The sources include:

- the results of 'happiness sheets' from learners at the end of courses;
- direct feedback from people to whom you are providing mentoring and coaching;
- direct feedback from your manager;
- direct feedback from learners in conversations during courses;
- personal benchmarks against acknowledged excellent trainers.

This personal development checklist should be honestly scored, giving a mark out of 10 for each point. Over a number of months, check the improvement in the overall total and individual scores. Those scores that continue to be consistently low highlight the areas of performance that need improvement.

This approach will constantly remind the trainer of the importance of self-evaluation, and also of the importance of personal learning. Trainers should be ready to benchmark themselves against colleagues and against external trainers, and should seek to find time in their busy schedules to attend courses within the organization as well as external ones.

Establishing appropriate standards

This chapter has been devoted to key aspects of evaluation in HR/OD/ L&D/Training departments. Such evaluation only has meaning when it is done against meaningful, agreed standards. Some of the measurement standards are straightforward. For example, a standard could be set that a trainer should undertake at least 100 days of delivering training programmes in a year. However, at the other extreme you may wish to evaluate situations where standards are very difficult to express. What would be a standard that could evaluate the contribution of an individual course to the business success of the organization?

In between these two extremes there are standards in regular use about which there is significant debate. If a standard is set that a trainer should regularly be achieving a mark of at least 90 per cent learner satisfaction on a 'happiness sheet', what does that mean? Is such a standard realistic given the environment in which the course is being given? Was it realistic last week? Will it be realistic next week? Standards in HR/OD/L&D/ Training are vital and necessary, but not always easy to implement. They will always be a mixture of 'hard' and 'soft'. The vital concerns are that the standards are set and are agreed as being realistic for the overall good of the trainer, the HR/OD/L&D/Training function, the learners and the organization.

Appendix 1 contains areas of learning and development to which evaluation procedures could be applied.

Checklist for trainer's personal evaluation

✔ What are the key skills, knowledge and behaviours for a trainer?
✔ What is the mix of these abilities in those trainers who are widely regarded as the best?
✔ What proactive actions am I taking to receive feedback on my performance?
✔ How well do I match against the best?
✔ Am I watching other trainers?
✔ Am I developing a personal checklist and a personal model of training excellence against which I can continuously evaluate myself?
✔ How well do I match against my personal checklist?
✔ Are my scores against this list regularly improving?
✔ What am I doing to learn and to improve?
✔ Am I using a personal development plan and a personal skills development plan?

Setting standards through best practice

Standards employed in HR/OD/L&D/Training have typically been implemented as the result of experience and best practice. This has generally been arrived at by cyclical trial and error approaches. Based on trainers' experiences a performance standard is set for a learning and development programme or for a specific learning event. As experience grows of implementing the training initiative and evaluating results, the standards for performance can be discussed and modified appropriately. In most organizations this approach to the development of standards has occurred with little conscious planning. However, these best practice methods are widely used and regarded as successful. HR/OD/L&D/Training staff should recognize the current standards and adopt the cyclical approach to continue to improve them. The team should be asking the following questions. How and when were the standards set for the evaluation of learning and development? Are the standards still appropriate? Are they regularly being updated?

Setting standards through benchmarking

Most trainers are familiar with standards set by some form of best practice approach. For many organizations this is in fact sufficient; the agreed internal standards for training and development are accepted as being appropriate for all evaluation needs. However, other organizations are attempting to set standards for key functions, including HR/OD/L&D/Training, through benchmarking against acknowledged excellence.

Benchmarking with other organizations

Benchmarking all aspects of training and development, including evaluation, is in reality quite challenging. There is much published material about the results of benchmarking and about the implementation of training excellence; the evidence tends to be qualitative. For standards to be established through benchmarking you also need sets of quantitative data, and these are difficult to assemble. To handle this, trainers need to be proactive in their benchmarking initiatives, and the following provides a useful approach.

Use your personal experience, recently published articles and your personal network to develop a picture of the trends and important issues in training and development, particularly in the arena of evaluation. This will build your own knowledge of evaluation in training and development and build your credibility to undertake the next steps.

Enquire within your own organization if external benchmarking is already employed on other topics; find out which external organizations may welcome benchmarking initiatives.

Approach the management of HR/OD/L&D/Training functions in organizations geographically close to you. Ask if they would be prepared to share knowledge and views, and, if so, to what level of detail. Our experience has been that companies will willingly trade such information if it is not commercially sensitive. There is normally sufficient benefit to each side to make meetings worthwhile.

Be prepared to exchange information about the way in which you plan and prepare training initiatives and their evaluation, rather than the actual content. This will be less likely to cause commercial embarrassment to either side.

In some commercial fields there are networks of HR/OD/L&D/Training functions from several organizations. These groups meet regularly and exchange a lot of highly useful information. They tend to be reasonably informal and are discovered by enquiring through your contacts in the industry. If such a network does not exist, you might consider starting one. It can be of immense value to your training initiatives as well as to your own development.

Once mutual agreement about the areas of discussion is reached, then HR/OD/L&D/Training functions can meet. The normal format of the meeting is for each team to make a presentation to an agreed agenda and for the meeting to discuss the issues raised. For most purposes a six-monthly meeting, perhaps lasting half a day, will be sufficient for each team to absorb a lot of useful information.

Ensure that the debate on how evaluation is carried out has an important place on the agenda. Discuss, if possible, how other organizations quantify the value of training to their business.

It is not unusual for these meetings to promote less formal sessions between individuals from different organizations. There have even been examples in which a number of organizations have worked together with an external training consultant on a programme that each team needed.

Trainers should be naturally inquisitive and want to compare their personal contributions with those of other trainers both within their own organization and with those elsewhere. This comparison with others becomes very important if a trainer decides on self-employment in a training career. Trainers may well be able, through personal networks, to establish a personal connection with a trainer in another organization, and through this connection undertake significant benchmarking.

If necessary, use external consultants to benchmark for you when the cost is appropriate. They should have a wide bank of experience and data as well as the contacts to undertake further searches on your behalf.

As you work to establish connections you will have to accept that some organizations will not take part in benchmarking exercises. You can try to sell the mutual benefit, but you may find the idea of benchmarking across organizations is totally unacceptable to them.

Internal benchmarking

Even if your organization does not have other learning and development functions with which you can benchmark, there may be functions that are acknowledged for their excellence, particularly for client service. Discuss with them:

- how they set up objectives and plans;
- how they monitor those objectives and plans through to success;
- what exactly is evaluated and the methods of evaluation that are used;
- how they develop their evaluation processes with their clients, internal and external;
- how, and how quickly, they can change programmes in response to what is learnt from evaluation;
- how responsibilities for evaluation and using the results are implemented;
- how they use benchmarking.

Final thoughts

Benchmarking is a powerful business approach. It does take a lot of time to undertake and the results can take time to turn into really useful information to improve your organization. When benchmarking evaluation, as in all benchmarking initiatives, it is really important to consider what benchmarked information would be useful and could be used. Do not be tempted into 'nice to haves' that will be of no real use. The section on aspects of training for evaluation and benchmarking in Appendix 1 lists those features of learning and development, including aspects of evaluation, that are worth considering in benchmarking initiatives.

Maintaining the standards

Building, interpreting and modifying standards for training and development are major tasks for trainers. It is, however, the foundation of successful evaluation. The standards that are to be implemented should be retained in a standards manual for the HR/OD/L&D/Training function, and an individual trainer should be made responsible for them.

The Trainer As...

Coach

Creating a coaching environment

The corporate world is changing quite dramatically, businesses are facing challenges on an unprecedented scale and the retention of key employees is a major ongoing challenge. Employees equally are looking for organizations that value their contribution.

One major way of helping all individuals fulfil their potential is to develop a coaching environment. This is not something that will be achieved overnight, but if you can engender a culture of sharing wisdom you are more likely to create a real sense of personal development. This is very different from the process of 'managing'.

A coach guides rather than manages; throughout history there have been instances of guidance being given by 'elders'. What if instead of creating 'managers' we created guides? What if we gave respect to the wisdom of our experienced workers? The very best supervisors and managers are those who share their wisdom and give guidance to new employees. The very worst managers are those who play it by the rules with no flexibility or explanation.

Introducing a coaching environment may have a very far-reaching impact; individuals need to think about their very best learning experiences, remember what inspired them and think about how they can recreate special learning. Managers need to forget about being in control, and instead help their team members to explore by asking open questions and being provocative. Although individuals should never be taken unsupported outside their comfort zone, they can be encouraged to push their boundaries beyond their normal learning experiences. Equally, trainers could also perform the role of coach and may need to recognize that in the future classroom training may become much more focused on the individual, and as a result small discussion groups or one-to-one coaching may occur more frequently than classroom sessions.

Traditionally coaching was something that might only have been offered to senior executives or fast-track employees. However, as more and more people become aware of the benefits of one-to-one support, coaches may be found operating at a number of levels within an organization. The new interest in coaching is also shown by the rapid growth in the number of organizations offering coaching services to the business community. Another major advantage is that if people really begin to adopt coaching behaviours, the organization becomes much more of a learning environment. People really do start to learn from each other, but it needs attention to survive, and this is one of the major challenges: in any large organization it takes constant attention to maintain any initiative. Too many employees are introduced to an idea, process and way of working only to find that it is not sustained. Creating a real coaching environment needs focus and nurturing rather than just paying lip service to the concept, and it needs ongoing support from the very top of the organization.

The coaching role

There is always a danger that newly acquired information is forgotten before it can be put to use. Once a learner has attended a training event, her newly absorbed skills, knowledge, behaviours and attitudes need to be reinforced. In some way what has been learnt must be rapidly refreshed back in the workplace. This reinforcement of a person's learning is one of the prime roles of the coach. The diagram on p. 155 shows the simple relationship linking training and coaching.

Coupled with this is the coach's role in monitoring everyday performance of his team members and in identifying opportunities for their development. Generally, the responsibility for coaching a team of people is regarded as that of the team's line manager, and coaching has become recognized as one of the essential leadership activities.

The essence of coaching is the development of skills, knowledge and appropriate attitudes and behaviours through one-to-one focus on the person or the team being coached.

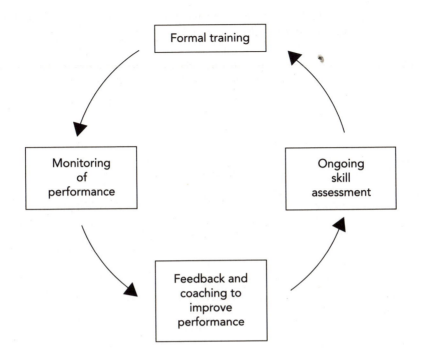

The performance coaching role

A trainer may be required to take on a coaching role in one of a number of circumstances:

- Line managers are not fully trained in coaching skills and seek your assistance in the coaching of their team.
- Line managers have insufficient time to devote to coaching of their teams, particularly when their teams are very large or geographically widespread.
- One person, perhaps in a senior role, needs to develop a particular set of skills, knowledge or behaviours but does not want to attend formal training courses.
- A small number of key individuals need to develop a new set of skills, knowledge or behaviours and there are no appropriate training courses available.
- To follow up a particular training event with individuals who feel they need additional assistance.

● To support e-learning initiatives should individuals require particular assistance (see Chapter 8).

This role will give the trainer/coach every opportunity of working with a wide range of people, of increasing her skills and enlarging her network.

Personal coach

What is personal coaching?

Personal coaching could be described as enabling, ie supporting, another individual to achieve that individual's personal goals. Within this context it uses a skill set that is similar to that of mentoring or counselling. To coach someone successfully it is likely that you will draw on the following: questioning, listening, observing and giving feedback; and will work within a coaching model of support and challenge. While this mode of coaching is often used by senior executives, the approach is relevant to anyone.

The difference between personal coaching and coaching can be elucidated by considering the concept of a personal sports trainer. The coaching offered very much focuses on the needs of the individual; it is driven by the individual and often looks holistically at the individual's needs as opposed to being purely work-related. You may also hear the term 'performance coach', but, while you may be helping someone improve his or her performance, personal coaching may not always be targeted at improving performance in a working environment. It may also be about encouraging a learner to be more reflective and to focus on behaviours rather than competency development.

Often a plan is worked out between the coach and the participant, which sets personal goals and targets and enables the participant to prepare for and take control of challenging situations. It is often very proactive, and the relationship is built up over a period of time, which enables the coach to develop a support and challenge approach.

Role of the personal coach

Being a personal coach is like accompanying someone on a journey; from this perspective it could be more accurate to describe the role as that of personal guide. As in any journey it is important to prepare, to have an overall sense of direction and then to build in special stepping stones. In acting as a guide there is the need to recognize that at certain times the individual will want 'guidance' and at other times will be ready to enjoy a process of self-discovery. As coaches we have a responsibility to get close to our learners and to help them to know themselves.

By understanding how people learn and building that knowledge in the people we coach, we are actively demonstrating the saying 'Give a man a rod and you teach him to fish.'

As a personal coach you will find yourself using a number of techniques, many of which are used in other applications, eg counselling, mentoring, facilitating and managing others. What is important is the way in which you use the right techniques for the right people, and also the way in which you build the coaching relationship, so that the individual is not aware that you are actually using techniques, and the conversation feels natural.

Right time, right place, right person

In the same way that a personal trainer would work with you to tone your body, personal coaching works with your mind and spirit. When it is done well the connectivity is seamless; your coach intuitively knows how and when to suggest meetings at times that will uplift you.

A personal coach will encourage you to step outside your day-to-day routine, help you to explore the boundaries of your learning, and support and challenge you at times of decision. The personal coach can be a sounding board, coach, mentor and friend, and can stimulate, excite and encourage you to step outside your comfort zone. Because the relationship is built on professionalism, integrity and trust, you will push yourself that little bit harder to achieve your goals. As with an athlete, you plan a training regime together and agree the times when you want to be challenged to test your resistance and personal strength of mind. Equally the personal coach will encourage you to wind down after you have put yourself through a challenging situation.

The personal coach will help you to visualize your success and to surround yourself with images and stimuli to fuel your imagination and to help you to recharge. The coach will weave in and out of your life, helping you to create a tapestry of experiences that help you to grow and develop.

The skilled partner will delight in your learning, and will help you to move forward with encouragement, giving you positive feedback. What distinguishes the experience is that it's different, it's memorable and it forms an important part of your development. Find the right time, the right place and the right person to guide your personal understanding and it will enable you to experience learning that is so profound that the memory will stay with you for ever.

The key point about personal coaching is that when it is done well:

- it creates rapport;
- it is set in the right environment;
- it is part of an ongoing relationship;
- it focuses on the individual;
- it shares mutual respect and the opportunity to learn from each other;
- it applies higher-level skills/competencies;
- actions are agreed and followed up.

So could you be a personal coach?

Your job role may be trainer, performance coach, facilitator, developer, internal consultant or learning designer. Whatever your title, your interest will be in developing a skill set and creating an environment that is conducive to working one-to-one with another person.

Only the first step

This section should be read in the context of supporting personal development for coaches. A book should never be a substitute for the process of developing the skills required in becoming a coach. There are many professional qualifications available for coaches and if you are offering coaching it will be important to identify your own mentor who can help you to develop your skill set as a coach.

There are a number of references throughout this book to the need to refer your participants to others for additional support. There are important differences between coaching and counselling; there may be times when you recognize the need for specialist support. It is important not only that you recognize the need but that you help your participant to seek that additional help.

Client confidentiality

If you are acting as a personal coach within an organization, you need to recognize the significance of your role. Where organizations have offered counselling support it tends to be supplied by an outside agency. Personal coaches have some of the same issues:

- confidentiality;
- trust;
- relationship with line managers;
- loyalty to the organization.

As with the role of the internal consultant, these inter-relationships need to be worked out first so that everyone is absolutely clear about the roles, responsibilities and boundaries.

Creating a climate of trust

One of the fundamentals of being a personal coach is establishing trust. Without this nothing can really start. In this context trust means confirming to the learner that everything that is said between the two of you is completely confidential. It also means creating a sense of care, empathy and total professionalism. This is the foundation of the whole relationship. It means reassuring learners that their thoughts, hopes, dreams and aspirations are safe with you. It means that through your actions and the way that you conduct the relationship they feel confident in your ability to work with them and support them. It also means that you keep your own concerns, worries and views to yourself and don't use the sessions for your own gain.

It is also important to recognize that trust, once betrayed, is highly unlikely ever to be regained, so do everything in your power to maintain it. Never ever repeat anything that is said to you in a coaching session to anyone else, however professional or trustworthy you believe that person to be. Once you have shared what the learner has said, you no longer have any control over how it is used or repeated and you have broken the confidence of the learner who trusted you.

The implications of this are highlighted when you find yourself in a situation where you feel unable to offer the right support to your learner. What do you do? What you must do is gain agreement about what to do next. The options may be to encourage your learner to seek additional help or to gain agreement that on a specific issue you will seek advice from someone else on the learner's behalf. The latter can only be under-taken with the learner's express permission and with agreement on the elements of disclosure.

In many ways it is preferable to work with the learner to enable the learner to seek support; that way the learner retains ownership of the issue and also knows what information has been shared. This has partic-ular relevance in workplace coaching where the coach may not be the line manager, but the learner may raise issues about the relationship between learner and manager. In this context it is always preferable to support the individual in working through the issue, but to encourage the learner to work with the manager to resolve the issue.

There may be occasions when you feel that your learner needs specialist help. This may be technical and skills-related, additional training, or counselling to help the learner work through a particular issue. It is very important that you handle this up front at the start of the relationship by clearly explaining your role, skills and expertise and how you would work with the learner to prepare him or her to work with others, but do not try to offer counselling within your role as a coach. The underpinning skill set may be similar, but counselling is a very specialist area, and only people properly trained and qualified in this area should offer counselling support.

Everyone is different

Everyone is different and gaining an understanding of the differences is essential if you are to work as a personal coach with anyone. This understanding is based on a number of key factors.

Each individual learner that you coach will be different, and you will be different to the learner. Recognizing these differences is an important part of coaching and helping others to learn. What is fascinating is recognizing how subtle these differences are. No two people will have exactly the same combination of traits, and in this context we should never make broad assumptions about different learners.

One way that you can help an individual gain personal insight is by encouraging him or her to build self-understanding. One phrase that sums this up is 'being comfortable with yourself', which is used to describe that inner confidence that comes from knowing your strengths and areas of development. With this inner confidence also comes an ability to accept challenges and to want to explore your personal boundaries and comfort zones. Without this understanding there is a danger that the learner may not be able to respond positively to feedback from others.

Finding your own path to the future

This section focuses on you as the personal coach. Your ability to support others needs to be matched by your ability to create your own development programme. By charting your own path to the future you create a very tangible means of empathizing with the development needs of the individuals you work with. Identifying personal goals and setting milestone plans for yourself will give you an intrinsic understanding of the issues and challenges faced by those you coach. This is not to oversimplify the process, but much of the personal coaching process is based on a commonsense approach to setting goals and planning a route to achieve them.

How people learn

One of the most important aspects of personal coaching is recognizing the different needs of individual learners. This may have a real impact on not only how you coach but also whom you coach. Teachers, lecturers, trainers and workplace coaches may feel they have less choice in whom they work with, and there will be those who argue that coaching is a technique that once learnt can be applied with any combination of learners.

However, if you recall the people who have really influenced your learning, it is very likely that there were very strong linkages between the way they taught you and the way that you wanted to learn. If we extend this into the context of personal coaching, it is even more likely that an effective coaching relationship is built on something other than just the pure techniques of coaching. One of the most important places to start is to develop as full as possible an understanding of how people learn and to recognize the key influences and research in this area.

One of the most enduring models of learning is Kolb's learning cycle, in which he identified the key steps in how people learn (see Chapter 3). If your learners enjoy the learning experience, they are more likely to learn and remember. If they are told they need to learn something, their willingness to learn will depend on the respect that they have for the person telling them and their desire to learn. If their desire to learn is driven by a personal curiosity and they learn in a way that reflects their preferred learning style, it is likely that their own enthusiasm and interest will make the learning more meaningful and memorable.

Ask yourself and your learners the following questions:

- Have I created the right place for me to learn?
- Do I take responsibility for my learning?
- Do I use my preferred learning styles?
- Can I learn despite poor teaching? Do I seek additional coaching?
- Am I actively involved in the learning process?
- Can I learn in many different ways? Do I know what I need to memorize, what I need to understand and what I need to learn by doing?

- Do I seek feedback on my learning and performance?
- Do I learn from my mistakes?
- Do I regularly take a break and do something else to energize me?
- Do I share and celebrate my successes in learning?

Reflecting on learning

An important part of your role is to help your learners review the outcomes of their development activities. Encourage them to ask themselves the following after a learning event:

- What went well? Why?
- What could have gone better? Why?
- How could I improve next time?
- What have I learnt?
- How will I use this learning in the future?

Helping you to help others

There are so many ways in which you can develop your own skill set to enable you to help others. The very nature of personal coaching is based on the traditional ways that people have always learnt. There are the underpinning skills of effective communication, observing, questioning, listening and giving feedback, but there is also a range of other techniques and ways in which you can help individuals explore their own development.

Identifying your own style

Always recognize where your learners are starting from. You may develop a richer and deeper understanding of how people learn and their personal motivation, and may explore new philosophies and alternative ways of working. Assimilate this knowledge and use it to heighten your own understanding, but never use your learner as a guinea pig on whom to test your half-formed theories. A little knowledge can indeed be a dangerous thing, and any reputable theory of development should have either an accreditation or a practitioner development programme.

Inviting feedback

Who gives you feedback? Do you invite it? Do you believe it? As professionals, we should be able to ask for and absorb feedback into our ongoing development. Unfortunately there are very few people who are really skilled at giving it. If you are training people to assess or coach, you will recognize the importance of doing it properly. It is one area that consistently causes problems in organizations: so many people give feedback that is unhelpful during appraisals or performance management sessions. With less opportunity for training, there are ever more instances of unskilled feedback.

If you do develop a clear understanding of your strengths, you are better able to help people give you feedback. By asking the right questions, you will be able to elicit information about your own performance. You will also, if you develop experience as a communicator, be able to identify other people's responses to you. There are several references to giving effective feedback in this book, but as a personal coach you really do need to consider feedback in a number of contexts:

- How effective am I at giving feedback? How do I know? How could I check my understanding?
- Do I ask for feedback? If yes, with what result? If no, what positive actions can I take to overcome this?
- Who do I really trust to help me explore the areas where I feel less confident?
- How can I enhance my skills in giving feedback?
- What would I like to do differently when giving feedback?

These questions are intended as prompts, but as part of your personal development you may want to explore them in more depth with your own personal coach or mentor.

Selecting your own personal coach

A personal coach is more than someone you can turn to for help or advice. This person is different from your parents, partner, lover or best friend. This is someone who endures over time, will listen to your ideas, will help you talk through your deepest concerns and ultimately will allow you to make up your own mind. What personal coaches really do is provide a sounding board. You respect them for their views and they are a great source of inspiration. The nature of the relationship ought to be formalized, and there should be an agreement between you so that you are both aware of your responsibilities.

This will apply equally when you are offering personal coaching to others. They and you, as a personal coach, should adhere to a code of practice. There should be a duty of care so that, when you are being coached and when you are coaching others, everyone recognizes the full level of responsibility and acts accordingly.

Think carefully about who you choose as a personal coach, particularly if you are offering personal coaching to others. Do not simply make an informal arrangement with a colleague because you know each other and you get on well. If you are serious about your personal growth you need to identify someone who will stretch you and help you to develop new skills. The more experienced you are, the longer it may take to find the right person. The following checklist may help you make that choice.

Checklist for choosing a personal coach

✔ Do you trust the person?

✔ Do you respect the person's opinion?

✔ Does the person have the time to meet you?

✔ How has the person developed personal expertise? Is the person actively developing his or her own potential?

✔ Can you relax with the person?

✔ Could the person help you to set SMART and stretching goals?

✔ Could the person help you to develop new skills and knowledge?

✔ Could the person inspire you to persevere when the going gets tough?

✔ Could the person help you to grow your network?

✔ Would your life be less enriched without the person?

The best coaches fill you with enthusiasm. You feel better for spending time with them or talking on the telephone to them. We often identify them over a period of time; what distinguishes them from our friends, family or colleagues is their wisdom and our respect for them. We feel comfortable with them, we accept the challenges they set us and we want them to be proud of us.

Could you be a personal coach?

As discussed earlier, the role of personal coach has evolved from the principles of a variety of forms of coaching. What is really important is not attempting to work as a personal coach without developing competence. Equally important is recognizing the boundaries. In the context of personal coaching within this book it is about developing the competence to help people help themselves.

It is about skilfully using observation, questioning, listening and giving feedback to enable learners to take their own journey of discovery. The emphasis should always be on what they are going to do to take ownership of their journey, and your role will be one of personal guide, sounding board and helping them to explore options and choices.

What is different about personal coaching is that it is personal, and as such it should focus completely on the individual learner. You can help learners to understand how they relate to others and why that interconnectivity works better with some people than with others. By enabling learners to discover their uniqueness you can also help them to enjoy and reflect on the synergy of their relationships with others.

Recognizing your own boundaries

As a personal coach you should recognize a number of boundaries. The first is about encouraging learners to take responsibility for their own decisions. This is a fundamental point, which not only reflects your own professionalism but is critical for the individual. Although you may work very closely with individual learners, you must never make their decisions for them.

Another important boundary is the difference between coaching and counselling. You may in your work with individuals reach a point where they are in need of counselling support. Always help them to seek this specialist help; do not attempt to offer it yourself. Even if you are a trained counsellor you need to recognize how the nature of your coaching relationship may change if you also offer counselling support to the same learner.

Setting your own development plan

One of the critical learning points for individuals is the realization that they are in fact in control of their own destiny. When you help people on their own particular journey, it is so important that they recognize and understand the process and acknowledge the insights as they occur for them. This is another important function of coaches in that they can help in raising awareness of the stages in undertaking personal discovery, not just for their learners but also for themselves.

Finally, recognize what a special role you are developing as a personal coach: the self-belief, ability to listen to others, care and compassion are not just relevant in your work. Use them to develop and share in your relationships with others: your friends, partner, parents and children.

The role of the personal coach, tools and techniques are discussed in much more detail in *Personal Coaching* (2001) by Kaye Thorne (see Recommended Reading).

Using coaching skills

In each of the potential coaching situations described above the trainer/coach follows the same guidelines:

- Find time and place to devote full, uninterrupted attention to the person who is being coached.
- Give praise whenever possible in building the relationship.
- Be honest.
- Use questioning and listening skills to help the learner identify situations where he or she needs support and the new requirements for skills, knowledge and behaviours.
- Be aware of body language and any other signs that demonstrate that the learner is having difficulties with the coaching; be prepared to try a different approach.
- Clarify the points discussed and, when appropriate, note the agreed plans of action.
- Ensure that the dates and times of the next coaching sessions are agreed; coaching should be a continuous activity.
- Recognize when further formal training is required in addition to the coaching.

Within these guidelines trainers need to think through their own style for each coaching session and how it will match with the learner's style. Overall, the coach should adopt a supportive, encouraging approach.

Be ready to evaluate each coaching session and the overall coaching programme (see Chapter 9, p. 141).

Checklist for using coaching skills

✔ Have the coach and the learner agreed the overall goals of the coaching?

✔ Is the coach skilled in questioning, listening and feedback techniques?

✔ Are notes taken and shared?

✔ How will the effectiveness of the coaching be judged?

✔ How can the coaching style and skills be improved?

✔ Does the coach use each coaching session as a personal learning experience to review what went well, what could have been better?

Questions and answers

Q *As a trainer, can I be a successful coach? Traditionally the trainer's responsibilities have committed me to a full-time role in the training room. My impression is that coaching is concerned with continuous, ongoing evaluation, discussion and feedback. I may only infrequently meet the learner.*

A The trainer acting as a coach may not be in a perfect situation; he or she may not be as effective as a traditional full-time, line manager coach. However, particularly in the situations described above, a trainer can provide great benefit in a coaching role. The coaching will tend to be continual, ie with breaks, rather than continuous. It simply means that the trainer/coach very much needs to bring into play his or her questioning skills to orient each coaching opportunity. It is also especially important that notes are taken and used to record progress during and in between coaching sessions. Some organizations are moving towards more reliance on individual, desk-based, e-learning (see Chapter 9) in parallel with more conventional, workshop-based training. In these organizations a coaching role for trainers is of great importance for those learners who need assistance with newer styles of learning.

Q *In coaching a person towards improving their contribution to the business, how much does the coach really need to know about the business?*

A Theoretically, the trainer/coach needs no direct knowledge of the topic of the coaching. The coach is armed with coaching skills built around probing questioning and active listening. With these skills he works with the learner to unravel situations and to plan progress. In reality, of course, coaches will normally have at least a general level of knowledge of the topics. This will allow the coach to focus the conversation and shorten the length of the coaching periods.

Q *Is coaching always directed at one individual?*

A Coaching may well be with a team. The coaching may be with a team of the trainer's own colleagues, proactively helping them to develop their skills. In addition, the trainer should always be prepared to coach upwards within the organization. This involves the trainer in identifying with senior management situations where new training and development initiatives could be of benefit to the organization.

Q *Will it ever be necessary for me to break the trust and openness of the one-on-one coaching environment to bring issues to the notice of senior management?*

A There is always an overall responsibility to the organization in which the trainer works. Without naming individuals, senior management should be made aware of deep, repeated problems within the workforce that are adversely impacting on performance. The trainer/coach and the learner should both be aware of this. On the positive side, with permission the outputs from coaching sessions can be passed up the organization as good ideas for business improvement.

Mentor

The mentoring role

A mentor is usually nominated within an organization to provide guidance and insight to others, often to younger people who are new to the organization. The mentor role tends to be far less proactive than that of the coach. A mentor usually only provides the knowledge, guidance and insight on request. Mentors are typically experienced people with a high level of knowledge of the organization and how things are done. Often they have access to the really important people within an organization. They also understand how things can go wrong and can assist their learners to cope with difficult times. A mentor may be appointed to a new starter in an organization and then stay as the learner's mentor throughout that new person's career. This will continue even when the learner moves from function to function and from line manager to line manager.

The trainer in a mentoring role

As a trainer you are ideally placed to take a role as a mentor, particularly when you have been with an organization for several years. Typically you have developed, through the training role, a wide knowledge of the organization, its aims, its ways of working and the key people. Training is often directed at new people, and the trainer develops a keen awareness of their needs and their issues. Mentors need to provide information in a digestible form or to translate input from others to reassure the new employee. They also need to be open, trustworthy, an attentive listener and a positive role model. All these are the typical ways an experienced trainer works.

Be ready to evaluate each mentoring session and the overall mentoring programme (see the section on the evaluation of training events).

Checklist for the mentoring role

✔ What exactly are the expectations of a mentor in this organization?

✔ Have the mentor and learner agreed the overall goals of the mentoring programme?

✔ Are agreements and activities to be undertaken in between mentoring sessions being noted?

✔ What measures are in place to monitor the impact of mentors?

✔ How often will the learner and his or her mentor evaluate how well the mentoring process is helping the learner?

Questions and answers

Q *As a trainer, what could be the problems of taking on a mentor role?*

A As with so many things, the enemy is time, particularly if you have an intensive training commitment. The key point here is to maintain your role as the mentor. Do not be tempted to take on the role and responsibilities of the learner's manager and of other functions, such as personnel. The mentor must clearly position herself as the person who is available for the frank, open working sessions of mentoring and not as somebody who will willingly absorb additional responsibilities. The trainer/mentor must be absolutely sure that the guidance given to the learner is reinforcing the objectives and values of the organization.

Q *What are the differences between coaches and mentors?*

A There are no real boundaries between the skill sets that are applied. In most cases the roles actually do overlap. Coaching is basically continuous and proactive while mentoring is more 'waiting to be asked'. Again, the message for the trainer is that both these roles can bring tremendous benefit in the development of organizations and their staff. However, both roles are time-consuming and the trainer needs clear agreement as to how much time is to be devoted to these activities.

Facilitator

The facilitating role

Increasingly, organizations are using facilitators to run meetings and similar events. The facilitator is the controller of the process of the meeting, and ensures that all the people at the meeting keep to the agreed rules and processes. This allows the meeting delegates to concentrate on the objectives and the content of the meeting.

The trainer in a facilitating role

As a facilitator you are there to help and ease the process. Using an enhanced skill set, you will work with the group through set procedures to reach a conclusion. You should have the ability to remain objective and to rise above the detail of the debate. Your goal is to enable the group to work together, respecting each other's viewpoint and participating fully.

Acting as a meeting facilitator should be a natural extension of the trainer role. An experienced trainer will normally be using facilitative skills in his or her work with the group. The role of a meeting facilitator is as follows:

- ensuring the meeting follows the agenda;
- ensuring the meeting uses the 'rules, processes and tools' that have been agreed for the meeting;
- encouraging good meeting behaviours, including full participation, no secondary meetings and the recording of commitments made by the delegates.

As well as facilitating individual meetings, you are likely to also be facilitating groups working together for long periods of time: the skill set is the same. As a facilitator you should:

- ask probing, open-ended questions;
- positively respond to each and every contribution from the group;
- encourage input from individuals;
- provide clarity in conflicting or confusing conversations amongst the group's members;
- draw out input from the group, redirecting comments and questions to other delegates and not interjecting your own opinions;
- help the group reach conclusions;
- be fully prepared to provide appropriate knowledge;
- promote and assist with decision making;
- take away the outputs and return them to the group in a manageable format.

Use each facilitation session as a learning experience to improve your performance and enlarge your network. Ask for feedback from the learners, the sponsor and any co-facilitators.

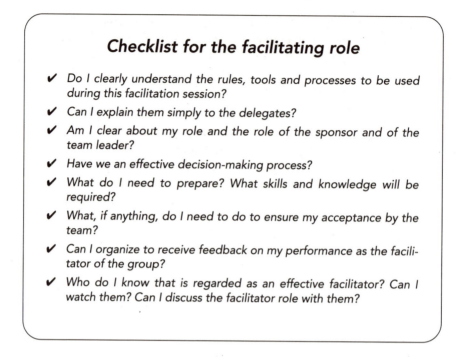

Checklist for the facilitating role

✔ Do I clearly understand the rules, tools and processes to be used during this facilitation session?

✔ Can I explain them simply to the delegates?

✔ Am I clear about my role and the role of the sponsor and of the team leader?

✔ Have we an effective decision-making process?

✔ What do I need to prepare? What skills and knowledge will be required?

✔ What, if anything, do I need to do to ensure my acceptance by the team?

✔ Can I organize to receive feedback on my performance as the facilitator of the group?

✔ Who do I know that is regarded as an effective facilitator? Can I watch them? Can I discuss the facilitator role with them?

Questions and answers

Q *Should I encourage being asked to facilitate meetings when I may well have a heavy training load?*

A The more ways that you develop and use your skills, the better all-round trainer you become. The disciplines of applying facilitative skills to a meeting will undoubtedly assist you in delivering intensive training courses. The meetings you are asked to facilitate may well bring you into contact with different audiences to those from your training courses. These occasions are excellent opportunities for building your network and your knowledge of the organization.

Q *What are the major differences for me between running a training session and facilitating a meeting?*

A A lot of the things you will be doing are very similar, particularly in applying the facilitative skills discussed above. The major difference will be the way in which you control the event. In a training course, standing at the front as a trainer, you tend to be automatically the centre of attention. As the meeting facilitator you are often deliberately keeping out of the activities, but carefully helping people through the process.

Q *How should I prepare to be a facilitator?*

A The answer to this is similar to the approach to starting out to be a trainer. Assuming you are confident in your facilitative training skills, a good place to begin is to watch an experienced facilitator at work. Then try to share a facilitating role with an experienced person before undertaking the role alone. Facilitating a group over a number of days, or even through an intensive meeting, often requires considerable concentration that can be tiring. Prepare as you would for a training session by getting enough rest and find a way to relax afterwards (see Chapter 2).

Counsellor

The counselling role

'Acting as a counsellor' has a wide range of different meanings in different organizations. In general, counselling refers to guidance given to people when their work performance is being adversely affected by circumstances that are not directly connected to the workplace. This guidance needs to be delivered by trained counsellors, who have the experience and the skill set necessary to deal with such situations. In some organizations counsellors are provided within a welfare or personnel department; other organizations rely entirely on external counselling services. To attempt to provide counselling when you have not received the appropriate training is potentially highly dangerous. We can listen, but should never provide advice.

The trainer in a counselling role

You will often willingly apply your trainer's skill set to coaching and mentoring. As we have discussed above, there are tremendous benefits in applying the experience and attributes of the trainer in both these roles. You may well proactively seek opportunities to coach and mentor. Counselling situations arise for trainers in a different way. Situations where there is a need for counselling are often thrust at you as you train. Delegates on training courses may single out the trainer when they need counselling help. They can see you as a caring, listening, knowledgeable person. You may be from a different area of the organization to the delegates, or even from outside it. These facts may make you seem easier to approach than the delegate's line manager. You can easily be seen as somebody with whom to share and discuss a problem. Similarly, there is a danger with coaching/mentoring sessions. As a coach or a mentor you are seeking to develop an open, trusting environment. This will enable you to work most closely with the learner. However, this environment could also tempt the learner to seek advice that requires counselling.

Whenever a counselling situation occurs, whether during a training course or during a coaching/mentoring session, the trainer needs to reflect the best practice. A trainer may listen but should never offer advice beyond directing the learner to his own line manager or towards the organization's personnel and welfare services. The trainer may well find this difficult to balance with the aim of building an environment of trust in the training course or the coaching/mentoring session. However, you must be very careful not to step across the divide into counselling unless you are trained to do so.

Checklist for the counselling role

✔ *How is counselling handled within this organization? What exactly should I do if a counselling situation arises?*

✔ *Can I talk to more experienced trainers about the ways they handle counselling situations?*

Questions and answers

What should I do as a trainer if there are a number of learners who seem to be asking for counselling?

Be sensitive. Identify how the organization has planned to handle counselling situations. If the trainer detects real hurdles to prevent an organization attaining its business goals, his responsibility is to bring the issues to the attention of senior management, but without betraying individual confidences.

Q *As a trainer, how easy would it be to become a counsellor?*

If your training style is appropriate, facilitative and consultative, you have a head start. There are a number of organizations that provide programmes to develop counselling skills and certification. The certification process can take several years, particularly if your study is part time. Be absolutely sure that you are committed to this direction in your career. In addition to the skill set, it takes special behaviours and attitudes to be a counsellor. Thoroughly research your personal commitment to becoming a counsellor and the possible routes.

Consultant

The business consultant and the training consultant

Often references are made to the involvement of 'consultants' in a particular business situation. When the business programme involves elements of learning, there is the possibility of confusion between the terms 'business consultant' and 'training consultant'. In our definition a business consultant is working on the overall business strategies, vision, values, objectives and business programmes of an organization. When the project involves translating business needs into training and development initiatives the work is done by a training consultant. In reality the tasks may overlap. The roles may be completed by a single person or by a single team. This section primarily concerns itself with the activities of the training consultant.

Consultative training and development initiatives

The traditional approach

The typical role of learning and development functions has been to respond in a reactive manner to the training and development needs of other functions throughout the organization. The relatively simple processes that have been commonly used follow the pattern shown in the diagram on p. 176.

Here there are clear boundaries between roles and responsibilities. The trainer has set processes to follow and owns each stage except the first. The trainer will complete each stage and check his or her work with the sponsoring function before moving on to the next stage.

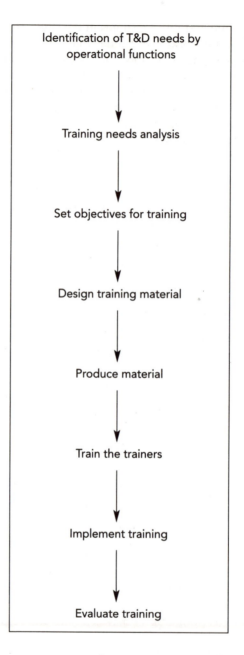

Moving to a more consultative approach

As the rate of business change has increased in pace, these traditional processes have often proved to be too slow and ponderous. Management has demanded large and rapid changes in the skills, the behaviours and the knowledge of the workforce. Trainers have not been able to respond quickly enough with the established processes. A different approach and a new training role are therefore evolving. This new approach, a more consultative one, is far more business-oriented and more continuous. It demands a wide range of advanced skills and knowledge from the training and development community. The new process follows the sequence in the following figure.

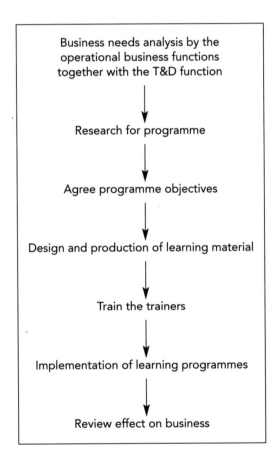

When this approach is fully implemented it is actually continuous rather than a set of discrete activities. There is an overlap of the key stages as the trainers work with business managers to ensure that the learning solutions meet the needs of the business. Its success relies on the close relationships between trainers and senior business management, and demands a very proactive role for the trainer. Here there is a definite focus on the needs of the business and the needs of the learner rather than on the training and development processes. At the same time there is an understanding between the trainer and his internal client to share the business risks and develop appropriate contingencies. In this context the trainer could be considered as being more of a business partner.

The trainer in a consulting role

To work in this consultative style the trainer needs to understand the business relationships and processes within the organization. There will also be the need to undertake an enhanced range of activities. The objectives of the consultative relationship built between trainers and the training and development function and the remainder of the organization is broadly:

- quicker response to training and development needs;
- highly flexible, tailored solutions to training and development needs;
- a high concern for evaluation and speed of response to required changes in learning and development programmes;
- proving mechanisms that allow the training and development function to proactively sell its capabilities to the organization.

In addition, the move to a consultative role will provide a stimulating, career-broadening role for trainers.

Marketing the training and development function

This will involve changing the relationship between the function and the remainder of the organization. The new style will be proactive, seeking to promote internally the offer of the training and development function. Management throughout the organization is made aware of the abilities, capabilities and achievements of the function. Trainers will make themselves available to present to other functions, and to work within those functions to initiate training and development programmes (see Chapter 2).

Developing a training and development strategy

This is the strategy to which the function will be working over a number of years. It is agreed with the most senior management of the organization and widely communicated internally. It generally will include:

- a mission/vision statement for the function;
- a statement as to how the learning and development strategy will be integrated with the overall business strategies of the organization;
- the values to which the function will work;
- a statement of targets and objectives;
- an outline of the plans to reach the targets and objectives, including the methods of learning and development that will be used;
- an outline resource and costing plan;
- critical success factors for performance and evaluation methods.

This learning and development strategy is totally integrated with the overall strategy of the organization and will therefore involve trainers working with very senior management. The whole document should be written in a few pages to allow it to be easily understood throughout the organization. The strategy should be reviewed with senior management at least once a year. The overall strategy should not change greatly unless there are fundamental changes in the organization. Implementation plans will normally be set for a year.

In reality, having a training and development strategy is not a particular statement of being a consultative learning and development function. Published consultative strategies are certainly no guarantee of how the function will, in fact, operate! However, the manner in which a strategy is compiled and implemented within the organization, and having the skill and knowledge to write such a strategy, is a true test of a consultative trainer.

Benchmarking the HR/OD/L&D/Training function

A function that is working in this new, proactive manner will almost certainly embrace the concept of benchmarking itself against examples of acknowledged excellence. These examples will include other internal functions that are praised for excellence, particularly in client service. Benchmarking will also be done, wherever possible, with other organizations' HR/OD/L&D/Training functions. Benchmarking as part of the way in which trainers and HR/OD/L&D/Training functions can evaluate themselves is discussed in the section on establishing appropriate standards in Chapter 9.

Managing meetings

The training consultant will need to develop expertise in managing meetings, particularly where there is a lot of information to discuss and where there are many different opinions. There are a number of simple rules to follow that will maximize the chances of reaching a successful conclusion:

- Ensure the meeting is appropriate, particularly if you are seeking agreement. Are the correct people available and do they have the information to make a decision? Can decisions be made without gathering all the people involved?
- Keep the number of participants to a minimum. When relevant or appropriate, communicate decisions after the meeting to other interested parties.
- Prepare extensively for the meeting, particularly if you intend to chair it. Have your thoughts in order to bring each point to a conclusion.
- Do not let your views limit discussion in the meeting, but have your conclusions available when they are needed.
- Plan the agenda to support the objectives of the meeting.
- Notify participants in plenty of time; ensure they see the agenda and material to be read well before the meeting.
- Publish clear minutes and action items.
- Be prepared to follow up the action item list with vigour!

Risk management

There is a significant responsibility for the trainer/consultant to minimize risk as a consultative project grows. This is particularly true when there is involvement with senior people with whom high expectations have been built. The typical risks that the trainer should be seeking to identify include:

- lack of involvement in training and development by sponsoring management;
- conflicting operational programmes in other functions;
- lack of resources;
- lack of skills in the training team;
- lack of commitment to critical evaluation;
- lack of commitment to follow up by line management after training events.

It is not sufficient, however, for the trainer to identify risk. The consultative trainer will be seeking to provide recommendations for solutions to any problems and, having gained agreement from management, to manage the implementation of the solutions.

Other skills and knowledge

In the preceding sections we have discussed some of the critical new skill areas for the trainer who is moving into a consultative role. In addition, the trainer will be looking to sharpen the traditional skills of probing questions and active listening. To these need to be added the consultative skills of influencing, negotiating and coaching. There are also regular trainer skills that may need to be upgraded in the new role, particularly as the trainer works with more senior people. These include report writing, facilitating, brainstorming and presenting.

These new, consultative activities will necessitate the trainer building a higher level of general business skills. These need to be applied in developing a closer understanding of the business of the organization for which they work. Another development area for trainers is management of change, which we examine in more detail in the next section.

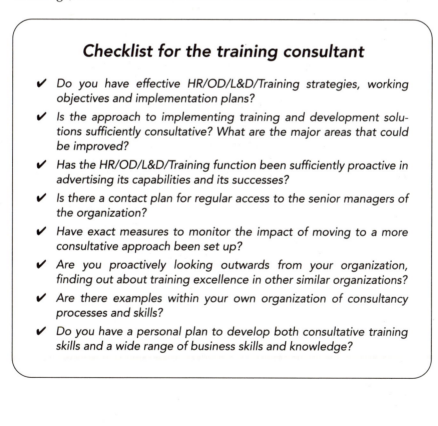

Checklist for the training consultant

✔ Do you have effective HR/OD/L&D/Training strategies, working objectives and implementation plans?

✔ Is the approach to implementing training and development solutions sufficiently consultative? What are the major areas that could be improved?

✔ Has the HR/OD/L&D/Training function been sufficiently proactive in advertising its capabilities and its successes?

✔ Is there a contact plan for regular access to the senior managers of the organization?

✔ Have exact measures to monitor the impact of moving to a more consultative approach been set up?

✔ Are you proactively looking outwards from your organization, finding out about training excellence in other similar organizations?

✔ Are there examples within your own organization of consultancy processes and skills?

✔ Do you have a personal plan to develop both consultative training skills and a wide range of business skills and knowledge?

Questions and answers

Q *Are there any disadvantages for me as a trainer in promoting the adoption of a consultative approach to training and development?*

A Some trainers have found the change initially quite challenging. They are moving away from the controlled environment of traditional training responsibilities and from the safe haven of the training room. It can prove to be quite daunting to judge one's performance against many more criteria than the familiar 'happiness sheet' and totals of training days. Although challenging, acting as an internal consultant presents trainers with a potentially new and interesting role within the organization. The trainers with whom we have worked in this way have all, given time to adjust and to learn new skills, gained significant enjoyment from their new roles, including a real sense of contribution to their organization.

Q *How should the HR/OD/L&D/Training function start the journey to being more consultative?*

A Actually making the decision to be more consultative is the first step. The decision tends to involve much consultation within the function and with senior management. This reflects the fact that the journey to becoming a consultative group will involve time, expense and, perhaps, additional external assistance. Traditionally, the journey has started by individual trainers starting to work in different ways. These small initiatives have been pulled together by HR/OD/L&D/Training management into a development plan that has been agreed with senior management.

Q *How long will the journey take?*

A As with all journeys of business change, the answer is very difficult to quantify. You are thinking in terms of three to five years, though significant changes can be made in the short term by adopting the new approach to implementing systems and by significantly investing in changing the skills and knowledge of trainers.

Change agent

In the introduction we talked about the changing role of HR/OD/ L&D/Training and with that change come changes to the role of the HR/OD/L&D/Training professionals. Professionals today not only have to be skilled in learning and development but also have to be business- and customer-focused.

They need to understand and be instrumental in the development of the organization's vision, values and practices. To achieve this often requires a new skill set, and a new language – re-engineering, transfor- mation, downsizing, rightsizing – much of which is based on change.

Rosabeth Moss Kanter, in *The Change Masters* (1983; see Recommended Reading), introduced organizations to the potential of change. Her book is recognized as one of the key early sources of reference for the manage- ment of change process. Since that time many organizations faced with increased competition and stretched resources have de-layered, stream- lined and transformed to become leaner, more fleet of foot, with a new customer-focused philosophy. The following diagram shows an example of a change process.

A Change Process

Establish vision/mission/values

Translate this into principles/practices

Set standards for individual job roles

Devise a performance management/ assessment process to measure the standards

Employees in these new organizations are expected to have a more flexible approach to working, to be willing to take responsibility, to understand how to work smarter not harder, and to develop self-motivated teams. For the average employee, supervisor or line manager this may present a challenge, particularly if there are no role models at the top of the organization. Handling change is not easy. People feel uncomfortable when shifted from the status quo, negativity grows very easily and there is often tremendous resistance, which manifests itself in statements such as 'We've always done it this way,' or 'I don't know why we have to change, it won't work.'

Taking risks or looking at the organization from a different perspective can be exciting, but people will need extra support to help them fulfil their potential. This is why the concept of 'change agents' has emerged; these people, once identified, work within organizations, fostering a positive approach to the business, working with, rather than against, management. They are a force that can be mobilized, rather like a hundred candles that, once lit, will illuminate a business with a new energy.

Companies often use external consultants to provide the initial strategic support, but there are excellent opportunities for trainers and internal consultants to be involved by creating programmes designed to help managers and supervisors coach, mentor, facilitate and assess. They can also help in the internal communication process. Importantly, change by its very nature is a constantly evolving process and trainers need to keep up to date. Daily, case studies are provided in the business pages of our national newspapers. Change is everywhere, and by adopting a positive approach you can be involved in exciting development work. As part of this work you may become involved in groups working on BPR.

One of the authors has developed a Motivation to Change profile. For more information contact kaye@theinspirationnetwork.co.uk.

Business Process Re-engineering (BPR)

The need for BPR arose because of the need for organizations to be flexible, streamlined, innovative, customer-focused and profitable, driven by increased competition and the need to do things differently. Most large organizations are not fleet of foot; their sheer scale, size and internal bureaucratic barriers mean that they are too slow to respond to the needs of their customers and the demands of the marketplace, and consequently a decision is taken to re-engineer.

What is BPR?

Re-engineering is defined in Hammer and Champy's *Re-engineering the Corporation* (1993; see Recommended Reading) thus:

> Re-engineering is the fundamental rethinking and radical redesign of business processes to achieve dramatic improvements in critical, contemporary measures of performance, such as cost, quality, service and speed. (p. 32)

They also give a simpler definition: 'Starting over, going back to the beginning and inventing a better way of doing work' (p. 31).

Re-engineering is often undertaken by external consultancies, and there are two reasons for this. First, organizations at the most senior level believe that they need external support either because of a lack of internal expertise, or because external consultants can be more objective. Secondly, external consultancies are more likely to have undertaken the exercise elsewhere and therefore can benchmark best practice.

Although the process may be driven by an external resource, the internal team have an important role to perform, because re-engineering focuses on processes, so input from everyone within the organization is important. Employees are encouraged to review their working practices and to identify more effective ways of working.

Although much re-engineering has now been completed, the ongoing impact is still being felt by many organizations. Experience has shown that BPR is often only part of what is required for business success (Hammer, *Beyond Re-engineering*, 1996; see Recommended Reading)

Organizations sometimes have not realized how far-reaching the process is, or how long it takes to undertake. As an internal consultant you can help the organization to view change positively by sharing good practice, using your network to benchmark and rising to the challenge of your new role as it develops, even if ultimately the level of change is such that your role actually disappears!

Assessor

Training programmes, coaching and mentoring are used to develop the skills, knowledge, attitudes and behaviours of the people within an organization. Within the organization managers and trainers need to be able to assess people's progress against agreed objectives. Assessment is about:

- judgement of performance;
- giving and receiving feedback;
- providing meaningful assessment reports.

If the assessment is to be of use, these steps are followed by a plan for an individual's development and ongoing assessment.

Generally, assessment of individuals and teams is undertaken by line managers and supervisors. Assessment of performance and behaviours is at the heart of performance management, coaching and the development of people. In some organizations there is a formal requirement to assess external qualifications against particular assessment criteria, and assessors have to be trained and assessed themselves before they are able to assess others. This assessment is about judging evidence of specific achievements or requirements. Evidence should be gathered in a variety of ways that encourages people to demonstrate their competence. It is based on performance, knowledge, observations and responses to questions. The assessment should be based on naturally occurring events, with support from realistic simulations as appropriate.

There may also be an additional requirement to reflect national standards that need to be applied consistently. To support this process training courses and specific awards have been developed for assessors.

Assessment guidelines

Setting the standards

Assessment is only meaningful against a set of criteria for performance.

This is true whether the source of the standards employed is a job specification, national standards or other measures. Both the assessor and the learner have clearly to understand the standards and how those standards can be translated into the everyday workplace.

Monitoring performance

A major responsibility for a line manger or a supervisor is to observe how people are performing against the agreed standards. In the traditional workplace, the office or the factory, this is relatively straightforward. Where managers and staff do not work in the same area, the monitoring of performance is less simple. There are a number of things a manager can do to gain information about a team member's progress against the agreed standards:

- Visit the team member's workplace and watch him in action, particularly in intensive situations, such as when he is working with a client.
- Arrange team training sessions and watch the team members practise their skills.
- Listen to feedback, both formal and informal, from other managers, colleagues and clients.
- Ensure that there are good monitoring systems in place and that the team members are using them in the correct manner.
- Review portfolios of evidence and test understanding through questioning.

Giving and receiving feedback

Giving feedback is at the heart of successful coaching and therefore is very similar to the skills outlined in the section on the trainer as coach. In summary:

- Find the correct time and place.
- Start positively to build a relationship.
- Use questions and active listening skills.
- Provide real evidence when appropriate.
- Have the learner suggest the way forward.
- Gain the learner's agreement, summarize the way forward and end positively.

Taking feedback on your performance against the established standards is a vital stage in your plan for improvement. You should actively seek feedback from your managers, your peers, your team members and those you train and develop.

Writing assessment reports

Informal assessment is often given verbally during a training event. Sometimes delegates ask for personal feedback that you may send after the course in a simple letter. Formal assessment, however, quite often will involve the assessor in compiling a written report. These may be to a standard format, with the assessor completing ready prepared sections on a form. If there is no form, the completed report should include details of:

- the standards being employed;
- timescales;
- the purpose of the assessment session;
- evidence of performance;
- an agreed action plan;
- details of future assessment plans.

The assessor and the learner will both sign and date any formal reports. They should then be sent to the sponsor of the assessment procedures.

The trainer in an assessor role

Assessment should be a natural process for a skilled trainer. The skills involved at the heart of assessment are those of observation and the provision of feedback. These are very much the facilitative skills of the good trainer. What can cause problems for the trainer/assessor is a lack of planning and preparation. It is not at all unusual to be asked for feedback quite some time after a training event has been completed, and this can be difficult if records have not been maintained. There are a number of rules that the trainer should keep in mind to ensure the information is at hand to provide the results of assessment:

- Establish in the planning phase of training events the details of any assessment that will be required and share this with the delegates.

- Assume that you may be asked for feedback during or after any event, whatever the original plans!
- Make short, discreet notes on delegates as you conduct the training event. Unless you have the most efficient of memories, this involves making notes at breaks and summarizing briefly at the end of each day. This approach becomes ever more vital the longer the mentoring or coaching continues, or the more delegates there are on a training course. Keep these notes confidential and follow the key points about feedback.

Formal feedback

When a training and development event is to include formal assessment of learners by a trainer, guidelines need to be established in the planning phase of the event:

- What aspects of the learner's performance and behaviours are to be assessed?
- What format will be used for the feedback, to whom will it be provided?
- What involvement will the learner have in the feedback?
- When will the learner be briefed that feedback will be provided by the trainer?
- Will this briefing come before the event from the line manager, or will the trainer be introducing the topic of assessment at the start of the event?
- Will the trainer share the feedback with the learner before the feedback is sent to a manager?
- What is in place to ensure that the assessment feedback provided by the trainer is to be properly used by a line manager? Are the line managers trained to use feedback and to manage performance and development?

The trainer as official assessor

As an assessor for any external examination you will be given very clear guidelines on the assessment criteria. There is also a support structure to ensure assessment is carried out effectively. This includes an internal and an external verifier appointed by the relevant awarding body.

Informal feedback

An individual learner may ask for informal feedback on his or her performance at almost any time. This is true on courses or in coaching/mentoring sessions. The assessment may be provided in the form of a private conversation. It may require the trainer writing a short letter.

In the case of a conversation the trainer will rely heavily on the notes he has made and on the use of the correct feedback techniques. Use the questioning approach to have an open conversation with the learner. It is important to support any feedback with solid evidence of aspects of the learner's performance during the event. This will encourage the learner's ownership of what happened and of what improvements are possible.

When a letter is necessary to provide the personal feedback to a learner, it really is important to be as positive as possible without distorting the truth. You do not know where and in what circumstances your letter will be read. Try and use the sort of phrases that include, 'You might consider thinking about…'

Questions and answers

Q   *On a training course with a lot of delegates, is it possible to provide assessment on individuals?*

A   There is a limit for all of us! As a general rule, on training events of only one or two days' length and with more than six delegates, real, useful assessment becomes very difficult. On residential events a trainer will have more opportunities to get to know the delegates. When the events include a lot of discussion or individual presentations, the trainer will have increased opportunities to observe the work of particular delegates.

Q   *What is the impact on a training event of the learners knowing that the trainer will be providing formal feedback to their managers?*

A   This situation needs sensitivity and experience from the trainer. If not handled properly it can lead to a difficult, false atmosphere. The best way of handling the situation is to discuss it fully very early in the event. Explain why the assessment is being undertaken and how it will be done. Even better than this is if the situation has been covered before you meet the learners, and this includes an opportunity for self-assessment. This may be done by line managers or perhaps by the human resources function. To encourage this to happen, make sure that all the details of the assessment are fully covered in the pre-course information.

Author

Why be an author?

Many people at some time have an ambition to become an author. Seeing your words in print for the first time is a very positive and exciting experience. However, behind the euphoria of achieving a personal ambition is the need for a totally professional and dedicated approach. There need to be clear objectives and sound plans. As with every other developmental opportunity, it needs to be approached in a realistic manner. Part of the realism concerns your talent. The most charismatic trainer may not be the most creative writer. There are some common elements in both, but they require different skill sets.

The publication of books and articles is one very obvious way to have your name acknowledged in the training arena. The need for views and information about training and learning topics never ceases. There is a continuing flow of new people with responsibilities for training. They are searching for sources of information on developing the necessary skills, knowledge and behaviours for their new role. In addition, there are many established trainers who are looking to understand how they can improve their skills and extend their career opportunities.

What will I write?

Having thought through the possibilities and the pitfalls, the next step is to decide the specific format for your first output. Is it to be a research paper, an article, a book or something else? There are many books on the key topics of training and learning. However, there are certainly identifiable gaps in the market that could provide an opportunity for your writing.

Writing for magazines and similar publications normally begins with making direct contact with their editors/publishers and offering a particular piece of work you have prepared. Once an appropriate article with a readable style is published, the publishers may well come back for further material. This is particularly true if your work has generated interest from the readers. Magazines normally have a schedule of topics that are to be covered in the following editions. You should start by offering to submit an article that fits in with one of the topics.

Getting into print

How to start

Whatever you set out to write and publish, you will invariably find that you will come up against time constraints. Initially you may be over-ambitious and try to address too many topics or issues. This will ensure that you will be struggling to complete the work in the allotted time! It really is vital that you approach the task with a real project management attitude, having clear objectives and timescales.

As you plan, begin with some very basic questions. The answers will give you the format for the project plan:

- What could I write about? What would I like to write about?
- Just how many words could I write on this topic?
- If there are gaps in my knowledge, should I consider writing with somebody else?
- Is it an article, a book, or an article that could grow into a book?
- Why do I want to do this? What am I seeking to achieve?
- Will I be able to write in a way that others will want to read?

Thinking through the possibilities

Having thought through the real objectives of your work, the next thing is to make sure that it is going to be worthwhile. There are a few initial steps that must be undertaken and a few vital questions to answer in investigating the viability of your work:

- Research the marketplace. Is there a space for your work? Has it all been done before?
- Is there anything new and special about your approach to the target area?
- How specialist is the work? Is there an audience? Are there any specific journals or book publishers that would be interested?
- Visit libraries, specialist bookshops, and university and business schools to research your topic.
- Network with others. Identify potential interested parties and share some of the content to establish their level of interest.
- Identify possible case-study material: all publishers, whether of magazines or books, are particularly interested in case-study material of individuals or organizations. Always gain permission from the participants first before approaching the publisher.

- Approximately how large will the finished manuscript be? What format would be best for what you are trying to do?
- Consider online publishing.
- Decide which publishers and/or magazines would be suitable for your material. Consult the *Writers' and Artists' Yearbook* for details of publishers of books and magazines (see Appendix 2). Think about the magazines you have read and investigate their criteria for the submission of manuscripts. Publishers and magazine editors are very experienced in working with potential authors and will be encouraging and helpful if your approach seems creative and well thought through.
- Approach your chosen publisher. They will normally expect to see an outline synopsis, a list of contents and sample contents. It will help your cause if you have researched the marketplace for your work and can provide information as to why it should be published. If all is well, you will need to agree the contractual terms under which you will work. Make sure that you clearly understand the timescales and exactly what is expected of you. It is difficult to be creative to order! Remember to leave yourself enough time to ensure you meet deadlines.
- If you are producing a piece of research, or a more academic paper, there are journals that would be potentially interested in the contents.
- Decide a pattern of working: how you will research, when you will write, type and how the work will be checked. Agree these with your publisher so that you can both keep abreast of progress and overcome any issues quickly. You will be working to an agreed time whether you are producing a book, a journal article or a research project paper.
- Constantly check your developing script against your objectives, your development plan and against the rules that you established.
- If your manuscript is going to take some time to finish, be prepared to watch the marketplace in case a very similar book appears in the meantime.

Checklist for getting into print

- ✔ Do I know why I want to write? Have I set myself goals?
- ✔ Do I have something new and innovative to write about?
- ✔ Do I have specialist knowledge to share with others?
- ✔ Can I write in a way that will interest others?

> ✔ Can I work to deadlines? Do I have the commitment to carry it through to the end?
>
> ✔ Can I write by myself or should I collaborate with others?

Questions and answers

Q *Are there really gaps for new books and magazine articles about training?*

A It sometimes seems that there are already too many books and too many monthly and weekly articles. We are so busy training that we often just do not have time to read what is already available. However, the training world is a very dynamic one. We are under growing pressure to develop learners in new, innovative ways. Our experience of working as trainers in newly changed organizations is growing. We are beginning to understand how a trainer can best contribute in 'flat management' organizations. We are gaining experience in how we can take a major lead in organizational change initiatives. In addition, there are an increasing number of people who need to understand the basic elements of training. This is as a result of the growing trend for training to be delivered 'in the workplace' by line managers. There is the need to report and comment on all these things. All these trends and all these new sets of experience are offering opportunities for authoring by trainers.

Q *How can I choose a topic for my first piece of work?*

A You will obviously write best about a topic in which you are involved, but for publication it needs to be something that others will also find interesting. You will be aware from the latest publications what the current topics are. In addition there are some topics that have become standard areas of interest for the training community. These include evaluation, linking learning and development to business improvement, and the development of the skills and knowledge of trainers and developers. Magazines will quite often be interested in your latest programmes if you are able to show at least the start of some business improvement in your organization that is linked to the training and development initiative. You may also become inspired about a particular topic or specialist area and find that the article almost writes itself once you start to record your thoughts. For further information on sources of inspiration, see Chapter 6. Think about your areas of specialization. Could you become a thought leader? See pp. 18–20.

Conference organizer

There are real differences between running a training event and running a conference. A conference will normally be an event with numbers in excess of 20 delegates. In the largest organizations the numbers may run into the hundreds. These large events require the application of exceptional organizational skills together with the highest levels of support. Planning in advance and a true project management approach are vital to success. The following sections discuss the key points to remember as you work to implement a successful conference (see also Chapter 5).

Early preparation

- Identify the overall aim/objectives; be prepared to reconfirm them as the plan unfolds.
- Identify the target audience.
- Identify speakers well in advance.
- Agree a date with the sponsor, identify a venue and book it well in advance. Keep careful note of the terms and conditions of the contract with the venue should it become necessary to change the details of the event, or even cancel it.
- Take care that your date does not clash with other events that could reduce the size of your audience. If your intended audience is international, be prepared to check national holidays across the relevant countries.
- Check if there is another event with which your conference has a synergy. You may be able to attract members of your targeted audience to stay on after another event.
- Design the marketing material, checking with the speakers that your descriptions of their expertise and experience and of their intended presentations are accurate.
- Plan the marketing using a variety of methods aimed at putting the information about your conference in front of those likely to want to attend. If you intend to use a mailing firm, ensure that it is reputable and experienced in your field, and that its mailing lists are current.
- Begin to think of contingency planning. Be prepared without becoming over worried! Keep a wary eye on some of the things that

could cause you problems, particularly sudden illness of speakers, problems with the venue, train strikes and so on.

Closer to the event

- Mail the information about the conference to your target audience, allowing a minimum of six weeks and ideally three months before the event. There is a delicate balance between sending out information with sufficient notice and sending it out so early it fails to register as important with the potential audience.
- Consider other forms of publicity, including advertisement entries in training and trade magazines, flyers in magazines and e-mail. In general, print runs of material should be organized two months before they are required to ensure that time is allowed for all the processes of preparation. Check the appropriate copy dates.
- Consider the publication of an article in a magazine that links to and advertises the topics of the conference.
- Be wary of your marketing spend; costs can easily become excessive in this area.
- Work closely with the venue. Identify the people at the venue who can help you to plan and who will be there on the important day. Find out details, including how messages to speakers and delegates are handled. Discuss with the venue management their experience, anything that could go amiss, and their contingency approaches.
- Continually, as the arrangements gather pace and the event gets nearer, put yourself in the place of the audience, asking yourself questions like the following:
  - Why should I attend?
  - What will this conference do for me?
  - How will the content help the organization of which I am part?
  - Is it good value for money?
  - Is the administration efficient? Will it be easy for me to attend?
- Develop a tracking system for the delegates and use their responses to form the basis of your registration process.

If these basic points have all been taken care of, the first registration should be with you within one month of the first announcement of the event. Be aware of the receipt of bookings in order that you can quickly react to numbers and the quality and level of those registering. If the numbers are lower than you expected, check the following:

- Has there been a problem with the mailing?
- Did we target (enough of) the correct people?
- Is the content relevant?
- Is there a clash with another event?
- Be ready to use the telephone to sample some of your targeted audience and find out if there is a problem.

At a set point in time you may have to decide to cancel. Consider the speakers and their willingness to talk to a smaller audience or rearrange their diaries. The planning should always include an assessment of the cost and the implications of having to cancel. If a cancellation is necessary, make absolutely sure it is handled in the most professional way possible.

Work with your speakers, ensuring your expectations of their presentations coincide with theirs. Thoroughly brief them on your expectations of the venue and of any delegate response. Are they to be accommodated overnight? Who will meet them and join them for dinner? Do you want them to attend the whole of the conference? Will there be a question panel at the end of the day you want them to attend?

All these things are vital if you are using external speakers whom you may be paying. These points are equally important when you ask senior people from within your own organization to present.

The days before the event

Make all the final checks of the most important aspects, particularly:

- the venue, including catering and similar arrangements;
- speakers;
- equipment;
- any press or magazines that you have invited to attend.

Hopefully, everything will be going to plan, but your well-established contingency plans may just come into their own!

Do all you can to be relaxed. On the day you will probably be under considerable pressure. The better you prepare yourself, the more able you will be to handle difficult situations.

On the day

All should go well if everything has been well planned. You will need and deserve a little luck for everything to be perfect! Spend your day with the speakers and any key delegates. Leave the arrangements to the venue management – they should be able to make things happen correctly.

After the event

Continue to do everything in the professional way in which you planned and implemented the conference:

- Thank the speakers, the venue and any members of the press.
- Follow up on any actions and plans that had been discussed.
- Analyse all the things you planned and everything that happened. What could be done better next time?

A training business

The first steps

Running a training business has a lot in common with being a retailer. Anybody can open a shop, but how long will it trade? Will it be capable of building client loyalty? Will it be possible to run it at a worthwhile profit?

At some stage in your career as a trainer you may well decide that you want to manage your own training business. Such a venture can be worthwhile, rewarding and fun. However, as with all of life's major decisions, deciding to start a training company should not be undertaken without careful thought and planning. In common with any potentially self-employed person you need to assess carefully every aspect of running a business. Importantly, you need to assess whether you want to run a business, or just want to operate as a sole trader. Identifying which route you wish to pursue will help you in the subsequent decisions you make about developing your brand and your potential offering to clients. There is a host of specialist help available from your bank manager, accountants who specialize in small business start-ups, and Business Link. Try to build as wide an understanding as you can of running your own business, and talk to people in your own network who have already had the experience.

Why are you doing this?

You are taking a massive step. You should be carefully identifying in these early stages the reasons why you want to run your own business. Many people contemplate the idea of being a self-employed trainer and many are successful – usually because they have clear objectives and because they are able to make things happen. Unfortunately, others fail. You must establish the goals, both short and long term, to give substance to your ideas. The real accent here is on 'you'. What is it, in the face of the competition, in the prevailing marketplace, with your skill set, that *you want to do?*

Your business plans should coincide with your personal long-term goals, and they should provide you with work in an area that interests you. Without these guidelines, the task of establishing your company and your offer may become overwhelming! On a more positive note, this really is a time when you can evaluate what you want to do and what those short- and long-term personal goals should be. If this is your first experience of self-employment, you are about to enter an exciting and challenging period. Warn your partner and your family it is all-encompassing and totally time-absorbing!

Do you have a mentor?

The value of a mentor to a newly forming independent business is possibly even greater than in an organization. For the smaller business, those processes, rules and guidelines are less obvious, and the guidance of a mentor is really valuable. If your training business is going to be as a sole trader, initially your life will probably be a lonely one, especially in the first few months as you search for the elusive initial contracts. A mentor, with whom you can handle the loneliness, and with whom you can critically discuss plans and progress, can make all the difference between success and failure.

To find the appropriate mentor may prove to be more difficult than in an organization. Ask a member of your own family with suitable experience, or a friend who has already developed a small business. These people may be very willing to help but have only an outline understanding of the skills of mentoring, so agree exactly what the mentor will do. Build a list of the topics you will discuss each time you meet. Give the mentor as much detail of your business ideas as possible and time to consider the ideas so they can be ready to provide accurate, honest, critical feedback to your strategies and your plans. Most people who have a business background will have experience of training and should be able to help you work through your ideas.

Creating a brand

One of the most exciting parts of starting your own business is the creation of the brand. Your brand will consist of your:

- vision/mission;
- values;
- style and approach;
- service/product offer;
- measures of success.

If you have not previously been involved in a brand creation exercise, this may appear a challenging list. The task is large, but without it a start-up business will have a fragile foundation and a high likelihood of failure. The brand will be the real strength of your developing business. It will allow you to be most comfortable in presenting your offer to potential clients. In addition, it will be invaluable if you need to build a presentation to somebody who will be a source of funds. More information is available from www.entrepreneurbrand.com.

Where to start

The brand should reflect your total belief in your offer and, as such, should come 'from the heart'. When you write the details and when you explain your business to others it must sound genuine; you should be proud of your business.

Begin the branding exercise by examining other examples. Research firms mission, vision and values from large, medium and small organizations. Check to see how training companies express their brand. Jot down initial thoughts and ideas. Words that work for you will start to form and you will be able to write a first draft. Take a few days to work on this, refining the phrases and individual words. Does it sound appropriate for the training company you had initially considered?

Once you have a draft with which you are reasonably comfortable, become really pragmatic. Apply a critical approach to it. Can it be measured? Is it realistic? Can you believe in it? Can you explain it to others and have them understand it and believe in it? Once the description of the brand passes those critical examinations, share it with your mentor, with colleagues and with friends. However hard you have worked on it, listen with an open mind. If there is feedback indicating change, be prepared to 'go back to the drawing board'. Spending time at this stage can make the remainder of the development much more straightforward.

Choosing a name and a logo

This can present the greatest challenge of all. Many self-employed trainers simply choose to use their own name and add the words 'Associates' or 'Training'. Unless you are a limited company or a public limited company you cannot use 'Ltd' or 'plc' within your business name. Should you wish to be more creative and reflect your brand in the title of your new company, there is work to be done. Company names are registered through Companies House. Searches are available from company formation agents; for a nominal fee they will search to find if your chosen name is already in use. Companies are highly protective of their name and their logo. Logos and trademarks can be protected by patent; if you wish to search this area a patent agent will undertake the work for a small fee. If your accountant handles start-up businesses, he or she will certainly know the name of a reputable company formation agent. You may also wish to involve a design company in designing the logo. This can be costly, particularly as we would strongly advise that you choose an experienced designer.

After the design work, when you are comfortable with the logo and the name, discuss their impact with your mentor, friends and colleagues. What may appear really creative and different to you may be just too complex to others! A lack of time devoted to these early stages could prove costly at a later stage when you begin to produce brochures and stationery. Most people now try also to secure a domain name.

Identifying your offer

The overall offer consists of many parts, some tangible and others intangible. It includes you, your service/product(s) and your marketing material, as well as your reputation as somebody who provides quality training. This is an important part of your brand. It will involve you in a good deal of research about markets, the competition and yourself. This is time-consuming, but, in the same way as when researching a name and a logo, can potentially save you from critical mistakes.

Initial research

Market evaluation

It is unwise to progress further without a period of basic research. Just what is being offered in the market and how will it influence what you are thinking of doing? Are you building a training offer into an already saturated market? There are already many specialist offers in a seemingly endless list of areas, including assessment, training design, change management, outward bound management development and training consultancy. Other offers concentrate on particular markets, such as retail, health care or financial services. You need to be clear where you are placed against this competition and that you appear to offer something new and interesting. The research will be a major help in formalizing your offer. In addition, you will have learnt a lot about the marketing that is being done by other training companies.

There is another potential benefit from this market research. The evaluation of your possible competition may have identified other organizations that actually appear to match your own. You may wish to investigate the possibilities of working in association with them or even in a business partnership. This needs to be considered carefully and there will have to be a clear understanding of the respective roles. Both sides should be sure that the benefits outweigh the potential hurdles and business conflicts. Should you decide to pursue such a relationship, you may well have the first test of your marketing and sales skills. You will be selling to an existing training company the features of your offer and its advantages to the partnership.

Personal skills and knowledge evaluation

You will by now have at least an outline of your offer to the market. Now spend time looking at how well your current skills and knowledge can support that offer. What can you do now, what will you find difficult and what will you need to learn? You can gain tremendous insight by starting with an 'I can' and 'I need' analysis (see the section on developing new skills, pp. 28–30). Undertaking these analyses in detail and with a lot of personal honesty should give you real insight into the starting point of your venture. Talk through your views with your mentor and start to implement your skill development programme. You should plan not to over-commit in the early stages of the training business. Remember, people will be paying for your service. They will not expect to pay while you are completing your own learning.

Your personal brand

Your personal brand within your training business is just as important. If you are operating as a sole trader, you are the brand, and it is you the clients will measure. When you are developing your offer and writing your marketing material, you will constantly need to assess what you are offering. Can you actually deliver what you have promised? Are you reflecting your carefully thought-out brand? In a highly competitive marketplace with many organizations appearing to offer the same service or product you have to be the difference. You are the brand that builds the 'chemistry' with the clients to make you successful, winning business against competition. You are building in the mind of the client a picture of yourself as somebody who is genuinely interested in him or her and who really wants to be involved in a business partnership.

You constantly need to be appraising your image and how you are presenting yourself. Do you always appear professional and competent? This is a time of self-evaluation that goes beyond examining your trainer skill and knowledge set. The offer you are making includes your sales calls, the branding shown by your marketing material, and the way you look as you stand at the front of the training room. Working for many years as a trainer, or even as a training manager, in a large organization, may possibly take the edge off our performance.

Your brand needs to be reflected in literally everything you do and in every contact you have with a client. This can be difficult if your training business is to be run from your home. The telephone needs to be handled professionally. This may involve an additional line with a professional messaging service when you are not available.

Building the offer

The approach to building your training business is, in common with any start-up business, based around a familiar strategy:

- Crystallizing your brand in preparation for presentation to the market: logo, vision and identity.
- Writing the details of what you will be offering the market (these should be considered through the eyes of a potential buyer):
  - yourself, your style, your approach, the way you work with clients;
  - your expertise and your experience;
  - the possible supporting mechanisms, such as your network, your contacts;
  - the offer itself, the specialist areas, the measures of success.

- What are the business benefits that you are providing for your clients?
- What are the likely training needs in your target market?
- How can you express your offer as something necessary and exciting in that market?

Outline your potential market:

- market sectors: retail, financial services, etc;
- types of target organization: plcs, small and medium businesses, public utilities, etc;
- geography: local, regional, international.

Outline a first-cut marketing plan:

- To whom will you market?
- How will you market?
- What methods will you use to break into the market?
- What can you allocate to marketing budgets?

Plan a launch. Will it be an event or a low-key, gradual entry to the market? Can you afford something grander?

Think through your financial plan very carefully. It will often take three months to find the first real business, and it may take at least six months to receive payment. Once the business is up and running, establish an overall plan that is aimed at a regular flow of business and income.

Your training offer

With a background as a trainer it is likely that your major offer will be as a training consultant. However, as you undertake your research and seek to offer something to the market, remember your other skills. You may well have developed quite specific skills and knowledge during your previous career. These skills may enable you to build a more targeted and exciting offer than simply as a training consultant. Your exact offer might be constructed from an integration of:

- your specialist knowledge in the design and implementation of training solutions from items such as computer-based training or distance-learning packages;
- your experience of auditing training solutions;

- specific details of training requirements in narrowly defined market sectors;
- project management of very large, international training projects that may have included language translations;
- true experience with advanced computing techniques or perhaps training on the internet;
- handling the human resource implications of a merger/acquisition.

These special types of experience may well allow you to build a very specific offering to potential clients. Because it is specialized it will be necessary to be very clear in your marketing. It may take time to find your first business, but it is quite likely that once you are established you will do well. You could be in that extremely powerful position of making, and therefore dominating, a market.

Pulling it all together

There are a challenging number of key tasks to complete as you build your brand and your offer. We will discuss many of these tasks in more detail in the following sections. You need to work steadily through the stages of building the offer, but ensure you have enough energy remaining to take the offer to the marketplace. The overall process, from beginning the plan to the winning of the first business, can occupy as short a time as a month, or as long as a year. The time depends on many things, some of which can be very difficult for the trainer to control:

- the size of the organizations you will need to target with your offer;
- the complexity of your offer;
- any time you need to devote to enhancing your skills and knowledge;
- the urgency of the business need and your abilities to establish the need with your clients;
- client decision-making processes;
- early agreement as to contractual and payment terms;
- the facilities for implementation.

As we have previously highlighted, the successful trainer or training business will ensure that all the stages of the business cycle are fully covered. None can be ignored. Many smaller training companies fail when they are successfully delivering because future business isn't being identified and won.

What do people want?

The needs of today's businesses

The majority of new training ventures will not be offering too much that is different. You will certainly have little or no direct experience in your new business role, and little success to broadcast. To maximize the chances of success, there is a need for a clear understanding of what is happening in the chosen marketplace and what is needed in training/learning solutions. You need to be asking the following questions:

- What, specifically, are organizations currently looking for in learning and development?
- Why are these important areas? What are the connections to business trends and to organizational requirements?
- What are the accompanying trends in staff selection and staff development within the target organizations?
- What solutions are being bought from training companies?
- What are the most popular formats of those solutions? Three-day training courses? CD-ROM? Self-paced learning books? Coaching programmes? Online learning?
- Why are these successful training companies (and not others) selling their products in these marketplaces?
- What role are the organizations' training functions taking in the purchase and implementation of training solutions? What about line management? Purchasing functions?
- What decision criteria are organizations using when they choose a training company and a training solution?
- What level of fees are clients paying for the training services they are using?
- What is stopping organizations from buying training solutions? Lack of funds? Lack of the appropriate solutions from training suppliers?
- What is the impact of blended and e-learning?

Building the vital information

The answers to these questions are obtained from a number of sources. The closer you really are to understanding the answers and the business issues, the better able you will be to assess the needs of the market. You should be building data from the following:

- your personal knowledge of training from your previous experience;
- extensive reading and attendance at conferences and meetings;
- publications on training;
- every possible opportunity to discuss training in the type of organization you are targeting;
- e-mails and the internet as appropriate.

You should also organize a survey of trainers in typical organizations within your target market. This will take the form of a questionnaire sent to training buyers. The questionnaire is normally preceded by a telephone call to investigate the names of the appropriate people in each target organization. Don't aim your questions at commercially sensitive areas. Be conscious of how busy people are, and do not antagonize potential buyers. However, trainers inside corporate training functions are often prepared to complete and return a survey form if it arrives on their desk. Make things as simple as possible for those who receive your survey by making the questions multiple choice whenever possible. Provide a self-addressed envelope. Do not include too many questions, and ensure they are clearly written and unambiguous. Be aware of how busy corporate trainers may be; include the opportunity for the data to be share with them.

The results

If the research has gone well, you will now have a host of data that you need to collate into useful information. Analyse it for trends and gaps that your offer may be able to match. Most important, ask yourself about the reasons for these trends and gaps. Find answers to any further questions that may have arisen, and generally extend your knowledge. Use the telephone or e-mail to contact people who have completed your survey and attempt to probe deeper for information. Always be aware of the pressures on people's time. Establish that they do have time to talk before you take the conversation further.

You may, through your research, find that there is lack of knowledge in the marketplace about a particular learning and development topic. If this is the case, you could consider undertaking a benchmarking project in that area. This will provide you with a very strong reason to approach the training buyers that you have identified in your initial searches. It is an excellent opportunity for you to enhance your brand and reputation as a premier player in training in that business area.

Who is offering what?

As your research helps you to build a general picture of your marketplace, you will be finding out about other training suppliers. Some of these will obviously be competition to your direct services. Your calls and your reading, particularly of advertisements and catalogues, are contributing to your picture of these training suppliers. Continue to build and analyse this competitive information:

- What are the characteristics of the successful training companies?
- Are there any common areas between the successful companies?
- Are there programmes that all training companies seem to be selling?
- What type of programmes are being bought by many organizations?
- What level of fees are training companies winning?
- How are they winning business? Are they marketing extensively? How are they marketing?
- Could any competitive companies be potential future partners?

Setting a business plan

Establishing a business plan needs to be undertaken against a framework of these three questions:

1. Where am I now? This is an assessment of your current position, the people, resources, assets and cash.
2. Where am I going? This is the visioning part of the process. What are your personal objectives; why do you want to run a business? To generate a high income? To act as a retirement springboard? To leave to future generations?
3. Where do I want to be in five years' time? How am I going to get there? What are the milestones?

Your research will have given you the information to set realistic business targets for future periods of time. The targets should firmly relate to your overall goals, business objectives and personal financial commitments. It is important to be realistic in these targets, but also to be optimistic. You will need an optimistic challenge to keep you focused, particularly in the opening months of your sales efforts. However, be wary of being too optimistic in your first year, when failure can be both financially damaging and extremely demotivating. Do seek help with your business planning if you have not previously undertaken such an exercise. There are many books on the subject, the major banks have helpful booklets, and your accountant will undoubtedly be able to help. Remember, though, in every case you will need the basic facts and well-thought-through numbers before you can start to produce the plan.

The sales forecast is at the heart of your business plan. The other important parts are the marketing plan, a financial plan including projected costs and a revenue plan, and risks and contingencies. The vital questions you must answer are:

- What, realistically, is the amount of work you will have in each of your financial periods?
- How many days do you want to work each month?
- What fees are you expecting to charge? (Your marketplace assessment will help you with this.)
- What set-up costs will you incur? The purchase of capital equipment, including office equipment and a car, needs careful consideration. They are expensive to buy outright, though there are other methods of financing the purchase. Talk to your accountant.
- What assets do you already have? You can obtain tax relief on assets brought into the business.
- What other ongoing costs will need to be included? Just how much can you allow for marketing, brochures, advertising, etc?
- Can you provide any other services or products that can generate early revenue?
- Have you considered VAT registration?

As you start your sales campaign you will be controlling your business through comparing actuals with the plan. A certain amount of variation is unavoidable. However, if actuals move wildly from plan, examine your plans in detail to see where things need to be rethought. As your business builds, you will gain experience in planning your finances and you will be expecting to work within much tighter tolerances.

Marketing

Everything is now prepared for you to take your message to the market. You will have seen during your research how other training companies market their products and services. Although yours is a small training company, the marketing processes you may consider are the same as for a large organization. Take care not to plan to spend large amounts of money that will bring little return. Your intention should be to stimulate the buyers' interest, arouse their curiosity and to make it easy for them to buy.

So how does a training company, particularly one yet to establish success, market itself to its clients? Where and how should you be planning to spend the marketing budget? What will you be doing to check that the marketing plan is correct, and what will you be able to do quickly to make any necessary changes?

Your first goal should be to establish your brand as a provider of a quality service in your chosen market. The methods you can choose from are:

- direct marketing;
- telemarketing using a specialist service;
- advertisements in national, regional or local newspapers and trade magazines;
- hosting a seminar, conference or workshop;
- having a stand at an exhibition;
- writing or telephoning individual clients with a focused offer;
- using network contacts;
- meeting people socially through associations, clubs, etc;
- building a website.

In reality, the list is immense. As you grow your business you will develop a range of contacts from a wide range of sources.

Marketing material

Whichever route you choose, you will need marketing material. At the most basic level you will need printed stationery. There are now many franchised operations providing professional printing services that can produce cost-effective stationery. In addition there are many local printing companies. Always shop around and obtain estimates and ask to see examples of work. Consider one- and two-colour options rather than full colour, and always proof-read very carefully. You can also create your own stationery using specialist software packages.

In the early days a full brochure may not be appropriate. It can be expensive and you may not yet be totally clear about what it should contain. An A4 folder with the company logo is a good marketing vehicle. Into this you can insert details of whatever is appropriate for a particular client. Try and include details of your vision, mission and values, products and services, all of which should be reinforcing your professional image.

Direct approaches

Initially you may find that a focused and targeted mailshot to selected potential clients followed up with a telephone call to arrange a visit is the most productive route.

'Cold calling' by telephone requires particular skill, and you may find a professional training course helpful. Some small companies use direct mail or telemarketing companies to support them. This can be time-saving for you, but will be expensive if you are not able to focus them into your target market and clients. Initial contacts made by any form of approach need to be followed up by you very quickly.

General advertising

Advertising is another option to consider, though again cost will be an important factor. In addition to buying the space in magazines or papers, there will be the cost of preparing the ads. There are a number of possible types of publication from which to choose:

- Generalized human resources magazines that are read by training management. These are normally associated with one of the professional bodies (see Appendix 2).
- Magazines designed for the training community. These are circulated to training managers in a wide range of organizations.
- Local business papers designed to be read by business managers in your geographical area.
- The magazines in your targeted market sectors.
- Local business broadsheets provided by organizations such as the local Chamber of Commerce.

Talk to the publishers and to the magazines and newspapers themselves. Investigate their circulation, talk to their readers and find out if they are influenced by advertisements. Some magazines offer 'directory-type' entries that tend to be cheaper, but again you need to establish the likelihood of success versus cost.

If this approach is of interest, look at the style of the current advertisements and make sure your design is more professional and more eye-catching than the others. Recognize that a one-off advertisement will have less impact than a series, although this obviously increases the cost. Always negotiate on price for a series.

Other ideas

In addition to this traditional, paper-based advertising the small training company can advertise itself through other means. There are many companies offering to sell you promotional materials, such as personalized pens, paperweights and paper openers. These are expensive to buy and to distribute and therefore need to be carefully selected. They are, however, talking points and can be part of satisfying the overall need to 'be different' to the competition. Think carefully about the quality of the product and how it reflects your brand.

As the business grows, you should consider extending your brand through sponsorship, promotional products, exhibitions and other types of event. Always review cost against potential business benefit and always be conscious of any possible impact on your brand. Keep the professional image uppermost and ask yourself the question, 'How will this help promote the brand?'

Your most powerful marketing tool should be yourself. You need to take any reasonable opportunity of putting yourself and your expertise in front of potential buyers. These include many of the possibilities we discussed in Chapter 2 under the heading of personal development. As a trainer you should be exploring the potential of writing articles and books, speaking at conferences and meetings, and finding other ways of meeting people.

You might consider making yourself available for teaching at a local college. This might involve teaching day release or evening class' programmes. The financial reward is restricted, and the motivation of some delegates is not always high. It is, though, another way of promoting your expertise. It is also an opportunity to practise your training skills when most of your time is spent on the telephone and away from the training room.

Promoting the launch of your company

You will need to decide how your company is to be launched. Local newspapers, particularly in smaller towns, are a useful source of introduction. They will allow you to write a few column inches about your new business venture. The skill here is to build into the article something interesting and special about you or the company. If these special features can have a particular relationship to the town, the article is likely to have greater prominence. There is normally an understanding that you will also buy advertising space in the same newspaper.

Exhibitions

Another approach to the launch could be to take a supplier stand at the next business fair organized by your local business group. You may meet some potential clients; you may even find that your training offer is the only one on display. You may also consider a stand at one of the regular nationally promoted learning and development conferences. Examine very carefully all the associated costs, including the production of stand display boards, marketing material and the incidentals, including travel and accommodation.

Make your stand simple and attractive and be prepared to give away a lot of literature. It is often better to focus on one product or service than to confuse your visitors with too much information. Remember not to block your stand ready to pounce on potential visitors. Stand to one side or sit in a relaxed manner awaiting their questions. Encourage existing clients and friends to drop by, making the stand appear busy but never crowded. It is probably worthwhile having a one-page 'flyer' version of your marketing material for events like these. Consider sharing your stand with an organization that is not a competitor. You may also be able to negotiate a discounted rate nearer the date of the event.

Building a database of contacts

All of your marketing will bring you into contact with potential clients and with many other people with whom you will network. You need to build and maintain a database of these contacts. There are computer-based databases that can link directly into mailing software. In the early days of your business this may seem a luxury, and your database will consist of a well-organized paper system. The key elements to be maintained are:

- names;
- telephone/fax numbers/e-mail addresses; website details;
- addresses;
- details of contacts, meetings, telephone calls, any literature sent;
- likely areas of interest in your products;
- any other interesting information, including other networked contacts, training companies they have bought from, etc;
- an action plan, at least a date for a next contact.

Be aware of data protection legislation.

Reviewing your marketing

Marketing, whatever methods you employ, will be time-consuming and costly. Marketing your brand and your services/products needs to be maintained even when you start to win business. You must maintain the marketing flow to keep your name in the mind of buyers. Websites should be maintained so that they are kept up to date and details of special offers refreshed. If you are using your website as a marketing tool consider very carefully ways of encouraging your visitors to return. There are service providers who will monitor your site for you and provide details of the hits you have received. Equally, you must be able to decide what marketing approaches work for you. Be rigorous in examining the impact of any marketing initiatives.

Remember the importance of thought leadership that we mentioned in Chapter 2. If you find that you are developing a range of new expertise as a result of your work in particular areas, seek to share this learning through writing, speaking at conferences and generally raising your profile. In this way work will come to you because of your reputation and expertise.

Having reached the end of this fourth edition, we wonder what the next 10 years will hold. We have tried to reflect all the changes of the past 10, and to broaden the scope to include other parts of HR and OD as well as training and learning and development.

We wonder if there will ever be a generic term for the learning and development professional. We have used 'learner' for the individual, but those working with learners continually re-invent themselves with different titles. The title really is irrelevant: what really matters is the power of the interaction between the learner and the person supporting that learning. Do they inspire, fire your imagination and help you want to make a difference? We hope that this book will continue to make a difference to you and to future generations of learners wherever they are in the world.

If you would like to get in touch with us, we can be contacted on kaye@theinspirationnetwork.co.uk, and david@ccfocus.co.uk.

Appendix 1: Forms and Models

Surveying the Learning and Development Function

This survey is about your personal perception of the learning and development function. Your views will be added to those of other people within the organization, and the overall result will be a major input to the continuous review of our activities. Please give your rating of the learning and development function against each statement. A score of 0 is lowest and indicates absolute disagreement, 5 is highest. If you feel unable to score any point, please score the # sign. Wherever you wish, please provide any comments and examples that amplify your scoring.

Name .... Function ....

STATEMENT   SCORE COMMENTS

In my opinion, the learning and development function:

1. Consistently provides training and development
   appropriate to support the organization's goals   #012345

2. Clearly broadcasts its own strategy and plans within
   the organization   #012345

3. Regularly updates the organization about the status
   of training and development activities   #012345

4. Regularly discusses with other functions the success
   of the learning and development programmes in
   assisting those functions to reach their goals   #012345

5. Is prepared to work away from the training room
   to provide facilitation of meetings, on-the-job
   training, direct coaching or mentoring   #012345

6. Proactively sells its services within the organization   #012345

7. Is staffed by professional people who understand
   the organization, and who consistently deliver
   high-quality training and development   #012345

8. Is consistently measuring its own activities with a
   view to improvement   #012345

9. Talks knowledgeably about new training and
   development initiatives and how these could help
   the organization   # 0 1 2 3 4 5

10. Is recognized as a source of change initiatives across
    the organization   # 0 1 2 3 4 5

Please circle your answers to these questions:

How many times have you attended a course in the past
12 months?   0–1, 2–4, 5+

If you lead a team, on average how many days of
training has a member of the team received in the
past 12 months?   0–1, 2–4, 5–8, 9+

Note to trainers: This form should be modified to capture the information
in which you are most interested. Use language that will be familiar to
people within your own organization, eg you may wish to substitute
'learning' for 'training and development'.

Sample Course Evaluation Form (1)

Please devote a few minutes to completing this form. Your input will receive serious consideration as we seek to improve our overall performance and our contribution to business success. Thank you.

Your name: .... Job title: ....

Training course title: .... Start date: ....

Please circle the numbers to mark questions 1–10

1. The course met the stated objectives   *slightly 1 2 3 4 5 completely*

2. The length of the course was   *too short 1 2 3 4 5 too long*

3. Your skill development during the course   *hardly 1 2 3 4 5 completely met your expectations*

4. The trainer's knowledge appeared to be   *poor 1 2 3 4 5 excellent*

5. The trainer's teaching methods were   *poor 1 2 3 4 5 excellent*

6. The amount of practical/practice sessions was   *too low 1 2 3 4 5 too high*

7. Your level of confidence in using your new skills is   *low 1 2 3 4 5 high*

8. Your level of confidence to improve your contribution to the business is   *low 1 2 3 4 5 high*

9. You would recommend this course to others   *not at all 1 2 3 4 5 definitely*

10. The facilities were   *poor 1 2 3 4 5 excellent*

Were you prepared for the course? Did you have a briefing with your manager? What else would have been useful to know before you attended this course?

Please describe your feelings about the course. Which parts were handled well, which could be improved (in this case, what improvements)?

Would you change the amount of time devoted to any part of the course?

Would you increase or decrease practical/practice sessions?

Is anything missing from the course?

How will attending this course help you in your everyday role? Will it help you significantly improve your contribution to the business?

Do you expect to have a debrief with your manager after the course to discuss your reactions to the course? How will you plan to reinforce what you have learnt? What steps will you take to use the new skills?

Note to trainers: This is only one example of the many types of course evaluation form. The actual form is two pages in length, encouraging the written answers. We have found this form has been readily accepted by delegates and useful to us in evaluating our progress with a training course.

Sample Course Evaluation Form (2)

Please devote a few minutes to completing this form. Your input will receive serious consideration as we seek to improve our overall performance and our contribution to business success. Thank you.

1. What were your expectations before the course?
   Did you agree these expectations with your line manager?

2. How well did the programme match up to:
   – the published objectives?
   – your personal objectives and expectations?

3. What are your views on the course content?
   Were things covered in sufficient depth?

4. What could have been amplified?
   What occupied too much time?

5. Were practicals, videos and other materials used correctly?

6. Did you feel personally involved?
   Did you feel you contributed to the course?

7. Were there sufficient skill-practising sessions?
   Were they of sufficient depth?

8. Are you able to apply the course to your role?
   How will you use the course information?

9. Are you ready to discuss your personal activity
   plans with your manager?

10. What else do you need – training, coaching, etc – to implement your knowledge? Are there any other follow-up actions required?

Please make any general comments about the logistics and facilities provided.

Note to trainers: This is only one example of the many types of course evaluation form. The actual form is two pages in length, encouraging the written answers. We have found this form has been readily accepted by delegates and useful to us in evaluating our progress with a training course.

Personal Development Checklist

Skills development

In the training room

Motivating, energizing
Facilitating, communicating, influencing
Patience, adaptability
Monitoring, evaluating, improving
Giving and receiving feedback

Client service

Proactive relationship building
Understanding key client requirements
Reflecting requirements in training initiatives
Evaluating, improving, reporting
Assessment, monitoring, evaluation

Management and leadership

Coaching, mentoring
Motivating my team, my peers, the training and development function

Organization

Developing, implementing, using appropriate systems
Developing, implementing training strategies and plans
Developing a brand for the function
Advertising capabilities and the successes of the function
Evaluation, standards

Knowledge development

Training developments

Training and development trends
Change processes and training
Developing a learning organization

Training mechanisms, systems

E-learning and computer-based training systems
Distance learning and books

Business skills

Organizational direction, strategies and plans

Personal development

Building a network, externally and with business unit managers
Understanding availability of conferences, seminars
Reading list: books, journals, magazines
Authoring plans
Investigating work shadowing, secondment, transfer
Personal development plan
Co-training, mentoring, coaching

Note to trainers: Trainer in an organization's training and development function should modify this form for their personal use in conjunction with the personal development processes of the organization.

Aspects of Training for Evaluation and Benchmarking

This is a list of areas that could be considered for evaluation by the training and development function and by individual trainers. The topics included are 'how' rather than 'what' and therefore should be capable of being included in an external benchmark. They are not, generally, commercially sensitive.

1. The training and development function's ability to build and implement a strategy and an implementation plan that are integrated with the organization's business strategies and plans, and are integrated with HR processes including assessment and career development.

2. Working with senior and line managers to understand the organization's needs from training and development programmes.

3. The ability and willingness to use benchmarking of internal and external sources of excellence in improvement of the training and development function.

4. Agreeing priorities for current and future training needs with the organization.

5. Promoting the implementation of a learning environment and the personal ownership for development throughout the organization.

6. Monitoring and evaluating all aspects of training with a view to continuous improvement.

7. Providing high-quality training and development services integrated with the organization's business needs.

8. Initiating appropriate training needs analyses across the organization, integrated with a competence framework.

9. Publishing clear documentation about all aspects of training programmes.

10. Working proactively with line management to encourage all aspects of learning, including course attendance.

11. Proactively offering mentoring and coaching to the organization.

12. Building a high-quality training and development function with skilled, knowledgeable staff, within budget.

13. Proactively seeking feedback on individual trainer's performance from delegates and all other possible sources.

14. Seeking to make appropriate changes in the methods of operation of trainers, towards 'change agents' and 'training consultants'.

15. Adopting a blended learning approach.

Note to trainers: This is obviously not an exhaustive list. Use this list as a starting point to consider the areas that would be of most interest and benefit to you.

Evaluating the 'Reputable' Course: Your Personal Checklist

Before the course

What was done to ensure my correct attendance and pre-course preparation?

What was done to let me know about what was to happen both in terms of the course objectives and content and about the surrounding logistics?

What would I do differently?

As the course starts

What did the trainer do to ensure the delegates were comfortable?

How did the trainer introduce the course?

What commitments to use the new skills and knowledge were made by the delegates (a) during the course and (b) after the course?

Did the delegates get involved early in the course?

What did the trainer do to encourage the delegates to take ownership of their learning?

What would I do differently?

As the course develops

What were the strongest features of the trainer's approach?

What were the weaker features of the trainer's work?

What could have been improved?

How did the trainer continually demonstrate interest and expertise in the topics?

To what extent were delegates involved? How did they show learning?

Was there an overall pattern to the course?

Which parts of the course really worked?

What could the trainer have done to improve the weaker parts?

How were the slower learners encouraged?

How were conflicts resolved?

What would I do differently?

At the end of the course

How did the course finish? On a high note?

Did the delegates (re)commit to using the new skills and knowledge?

Did the trainer appear to have learnt from the programme?

What did the trainer think about the course? What did she think went well? How did the trainer think things could have been improved?

What would I do differently?

Three weeks after the course

What do I remember about the course? About the trainer?

What do other delegates remember?

Note to trainers: This is designed to allow a trainer to build her own checklist when attending another trainer's course. It is only a framework and the trainer should add any questions that are particularly personally useful in her own skill development. Use your form in conjunction with the sections in Chapter 9 on evaluating trainers and courses.

Trainer Pre-course Preparation Checklist

Pre-course documentation

Invitation letters to delegates, line managers, guest speakers
Co-trainers identified

Training materials prepared: trainer notes, delegate materials, exercises/practicals

Location details

Room booking: training room and breakout rooms

Comfort: temperature, air conditioning, light, acoustics

Food, refreshments organized

Equipment:
- Seating arrangements
- Training equipment
- Video, screen and films
- Flipchart and pens
- Overhead projector
- Computer equipment

Delegate materials organized:
- Training materials: exercise/practical materials
- Paper, pens, name cards
- Course evaluation forms
- Any corporate materials for use during course (eg annual reports, brochures, product details)

Preparing

Examine training material: parts you need to read in more detail

Timetable: any parts that will be rushed and how to overcome

Delegates: are they confirming attendance and are there any issues
Guest speakers briefing

Line manager briefing, discussion

Meet and plan with any co-trainers

Reconfirm guest speakers, location, facilities

On the day

Trainer guide available. Acetates/slides/computer

Room prepared to plan

Comfort: temperature, air conditioning, light, acoustics

Materials delivered

Equipment checked and working

Food, refreshments available

Availability of breakout rooms
Details of the logistics of venue and event available: fire drill, locations of food, refreshments, toilets

Ready to start

First acetates/slides/computer ready

Opening remarks prepared

Ready to discuss course aim and objectives, rationale with organization's business directions

Ready to clearly introduce self and any co-trainers

Ready to discuss briefly logistics of venue and event

Ready to build delegate involvement and ownership of learning

Lost Business Analysis

OPPORTUNITY: French & Willers, South Poges. Furniture restorers. Two-day time management training course for sales force

CLIENT: Ian Smith-Fellows. Sales Director

CONTACT SOURCE: Personal network; George – one of his customers

OUR BID: Two days' delivery, one day preparation all at standard price

Client commentary

NUMBER OF BIDDING ORGANIZATIONS: 5

WERE WE THE SECOND CHOICE?: Y

WINNING BID IN COMPARISON TO OURS:

Bid price:	Higher	Lower	Similar
Organization:	Larger	Smaller	Similar
Previously known to client?	Y		
Previous supplier?	Y		

First contact with client:
Client's personal network	Y
Supplier advertising	Y
Supplier approach	N
Supplier listing	N

CLIENT OPINION OF WINNING BID IN COMPARISON TO OURS:

More specifically tailored to client needs	N
Showed more understanding of client	Y
Demonstrated greater experience	Y
Contained more details of solution	Y

Showed greater determination to win	?
Showed greater flexibility in approach	Y
Showed more flexibility in price	N
Included more supporting material of interest to solution	Y

PLEASE NOTE ANYTHING ELSE THAT MAY HELP WITH OUR BUSI-NESS DEVELOPMENT, ESPECIALLY IF WE WORK WITH THIS CLIENT AGAIN:

Client said the decision was very close. Winning competition knew their client and his organization from previous work and therefore had put in a bid with lots of reference to the way the organization worked.

Most of the competition had very glossy brochures describing themselves and their products.

Good chance to win future business with this client.

Appendix 2: Useful Contact Names and Websites

This appendix is designed to help trainers build their own resource bank of useful information; it is not a detailed directory. We would instead refer readers to *The Skills and Training Handbook* (2001) published by Kogan Page in association with The Institute of Management, which is a comprehensive listing of providers and other organizations classified by training category, specialism, industry sector and geographical location.

Here are some relevant websites.

Associations/professional bodies

American Society for Training and Development (ASTD):
   www.astd.org
American Management Association International (AMA):
   www.amanet.org
Australian Institute of Training and Development (AITD):
   www.aitd.com.au
Australian Institute of Management (AIM):
   www.aim.com.au
Chartered Institute of Marketing:
   www.cim.co.uk

Chartered Institute of Personnel & Development (CIPD):
   www.cipd.co.uk
Commission for Racial Equality (CRE):
   www.cre.gov.uk
Department for Education and Skills (DfES):
   www.dfes.gov.uk
Department of Trade and Industry:
   www.dti.gov.uk
Equal Opportunities Commission (EOC):
   www.eoc.org.uk
Institute of Directors:
   www.iod.co.uk
Institute of Management:
   www.inst-mgt.org.uk

We have also made specific reference to the following:

Basic Skills Agency;
   www.basic-skills.co.uk
@Brint.com:
   www.brint.com
Brook Manville, contact:
   brook_manville@mckinsey.com
Tony Buzan Mind Map® method, contact:
   Buzan@mind-map.com
Campaign for Learning:
   www.campaign-for-learning.org.uk
Employer Brand Institute;
   www.employerbrandinstitute.com
Entrepreneur Brand
   www.entrepreneurbrand.com
Fast Company, contact:
   www.fastcompany.com
Honey and Mumford Learning Styles Questionnaire, contact:
   Peter Honey: www.peterhoney.com
Institute of IT Training;
   www.iitt.org.uk
John Seymour (NLP), contact:
   www.johnseymour-nlp.co.uk
Learning and Skills Development Agency:
   www.LSDA.org.uk
The Masie Center, contact:
   www.masie.com
Nathaniel Foote, contact:
   nathaniel_foote@mckinsey.com

Note: New websites are becoming available all the time; use a search engine to identify the ones that are most relevant for you.

Publications and journals

People Management:
  www.peoplemanagement.co.uk
Personnel Today:
  www.personneltoday.com
Training Journal:
  www.trainingjournal.co.uk
Tmag:
  www.tmag.co.uk

Other useful sources of information are the *Times Educational Supplement* and the *Higher Educational Supplement*. *Fortune Magazine* and *Forbes* are a useful source on US business. Trade magazines such as *Brand Republic, Marketing, Retail Week, Campaign, The Grocer,* and *Caterer and Hotel Keeper* supply information from the various sectors. The *Writers' and Artists' Yearbook,* published annually by A & C Black, gives further information on publishers and other relevant publications.

Theatre in training

There are numerous organizations providing a range of services where theatre techniques and actors are used to benefit training initiatives, including:

AKT Productions Ltd:
  www.aktproductions.co.uk/
As You Like It Productions:
  www.asyoulikeitproductions.co.uk
Crag Rats:
  www.cragratstheatre.com
Steps Role Play:
  wwww.stepsroleplay.co.uk

Appendix 3: Recommended Reading

Belasco, J A (1990) *Teaching the Elephant to Dance: Empowering change in your organisation*, Hutchinson Business, London

Belbin, M B (1981) *Management Teams*, Heinemann, London

Bennis, W and Biedermann, P W (1997) *Organizing Genius*, Nicholas Brealey, London

Black, J (1994) *Mindstore*, Thorsons, London

Bohm, D and Nicol, L (1996) *On Dialogue*, Routledge, London

Bray, T (2006) *The Training Design Manual*, Kogan Page, London

Breen, B (2001) 'Where are you on the talent map?', *Fast Company* article

Brown, M (1993) *The Dinosaur Strain*, Innovation Centre Europe Ltd, Polegate, East Sussex

Brown, P and Hesketh, A (2004) *The Mismanagement of Talent*, Oxford University Press, Oxford

Buckingham, M (2005) *The One Thing You Need to Know*, Simon & Schuster, London

Butler, P *et al* (1997) A revolution in interaction, *McKinsey Quarterly*, **1**, 8

Buzan, T (1995) *Use Your Head*, 4th edn, BBC, London

Buzan, T (2001) *Head Strong*, Thorsons, London

Buzan, T and Buzan, B (1993) *The Mind Map Book*, BBC, London

Cameron, J (2002) *Walking in this World*, Rider, London

Covey, S R (1998) *The Seven Habits of Highly Effective People*, Simon & Schuster, London

Csikzentmihalyi, Mi (1990) *Flow*, Harper & Row, London

Eikleberry, C, *The Career Guide for Creative and Unconventional People*, 10 Speed Press, Berkeley, CA

Friedman, T L (2000) *The Lexus and the Olive Tree*, Anchor Books, New York

Gardner, H (1997) *Extraordinary Minds*, Phoenix (Orion), London

Goleman, D (1999) *Working with Emotional Intelligence*, Bloomsbury, London

Goleman, D, Boyatzis, R and McKee, A (2002) *The New Leaders*, Little, Brown, London

Grigg, J (1997) *Portfolio Working: A practical guide to thriving in a changing workplace*, Kogan Page, London

Hammer, M (1996) *Beyond Re-engineering: How the process-centred organization is changing our work and our lives*, Harper Business, New York

Hammer, M and Champy, J (1993) *Re-engineering the Corporation*, Nicholas Brealey, London

Handy, C (1994) *The Empty Raincoat*, Hutchinson, London

Handy, C (1995) *Beyond Certainty*, Hutchinson, London

Heller, R (1998) *In Search of European Excellence*, HarperCollins, London

Helmstetter, S (1998) *What to Say When You Talk to Yourself*, Cynus, London

Hunsaker, P (2001) *Training in Management Skills*, Pearson, Canada

Jaworski, J and Senge, P (1998) Synchronicity, Berrett-Koeler, San Francisco

Kanter, R M (1983) *The Change Masters*, Allen Unwin, London

Kanter, R M (1989) *When Giants Learn to Dance*, Simon & Schuster, London

Kao, J (1996) *Jamming. The art & discipline of business creativity*, HarperCollins, London

Katzenbach, J and Smith D (1993) *The Wisdom of Teams*, Harvard Business School Press, Cambridge, MA

Kearns, P (2005) *Evaluating the RoI from Learning*, CIPD, London

Kirkpatrick, D (1998) *Evaluating Training Programs*, Berrett-Koehler, San Francisco, CA

Kolb, D A (1984) *Experiential Learning: Experience as the source of learning and development*, Prentice-Hall, Maidenhead

Kolb, D A, Rubin, I M and McIntyre, J M (1994) *Organisational Psychology: An experiential approach to organisational behaviour*, 4th edn, Prentice-Hall, Maidenhead

Lambert, T (1996) *The Power of Influence*, Nicholas Brearley, London

Mackey, D and Livsey, S (2006) *Transforming Training*, Kogan Page, London

Malone, S A (1997) *How to Set Up and Manage a Corporate Learning Centre*, Gower, Aldershot

Mayo, A (1998) *Creating a Training and Development Strategy*, CIPD, London

McCain, D (2005) *Evaluation Basics*, ASTD Press

McNally, D (1993) *Even Eagles Need a Push*, Thorsons, London

Michaels, E, Handfield Jones, H and Axelrod, B (2001) *The War for Talent*, Harvard Business School Press, Cambridge, MA

Morton, V (ed) (1999) *Corporate Fundraising*, Charities Aid Foundation, Kent, Institute of Charity Fundraising Managers, London

O'Connor, J and Seymour, J (1990) *Introducing NLP: Neuro linguistic programming*, Mandala, London

O'Connor, J and Seymour, J (1994) *Training with NLP: Skills for managers, trainers and communicators*, Thorsons, London

Peters, T (1992) *Liberation Management*, Knopf, USA; Macmillan, London

Peters, T (1997) *The Circle of Innovation*, Hodder & Stoughton, London

Peters, T and Austin, N (1985) *A Passion for Excellence*, Collins, London

Phillips, J (2004) *Making Training Evaluation Work*, ASTD Press

Redfield, J (1998) *The Celestine Vision*, Bantam Books, London

Ridderstråle, J and Nordstrom K (2000) *Funky Business*, ft.com London

Scott, A (1997) *Learning Centres: A step-by-step guide to planning, managing and evaluating an organizational resource centre*, Kogan Page, London

Senge, P M (1990) *The Fifth Discipline*, Doubleday, New York

Senge, P, Scharmer, O, Jaworski, J and Flowers, B (2004) *Presence*, Nicholas Brealey, London

Semler, R (1993) *Maverick*, Arrow, London

Semler, R (2003) *The Seven-Day Weekend*, Random House, London

Slater, R (1998) *Jack Welch & the GE Way -- Management insights & leadership secrets of the legendary CEO*, McGraw-Hill, London

Starr, J (2003) *The Coaching Manual*, Pearson Education, London

Thorne, K (1998) *Training Places: Choosing and using venues for training*, Kogan Page, London

Thorne, K (2001) *Personal Coaching*, Kogan Page, London

Thorne, K (2003) *Blended Learning: How to integrate online and traditional learning*, Kogan Page, London

Thorne, K (2003) *Managing the Mavericks*, Spiro Press, London

Thorne, K (2004) *Employer Branding*, Personnel Today Management Resources, Reed Publishing, Surrey

Thorne, K and Machray, A (1998) *Training on a Shoestring*, Kogan Page, London

Thorne, K and Machray, A (2000) *World Class Training: Providing training excellence*, Kogan Page, London

Thorne, K and Pellant, A (2006) *The Essential Guide to Managing Talent*, Kogan Page, London

Truelove, S (2006) *Training in Practice*, CIPD, London

Ulrich, D and Brockbank, W (2005) *The HR Value Proposition*, Harvard Business School Press, Cambridge, MA

Woodhouse, M and Thorne, K (2003) *One Stop Guide to Talent Management*, Personnel Today Management Resources, Reed Publishing, Surrey

Index